A TO Z OF WEDDING STYLE

KATE BETHUNE

with illustrations by
METTE KAADA

ABRAMS, NEW YORK

This book is for Lauren, who made the
most beautiful bride on November 16, 2013

Editor: Samantha Weiner
Designer: Reena Kataria
Copy Editor: Rebeka Russell
Production Manager: Kathleen Gaffney

Library of Congress Control Number: 2014942357

ISBN: 978-1-4197-1559-4

First published by V&A Publishing, 2014
Victoria and Albert Museum
South Kensington
London sw 7 2rl
www.vandapublishing.com

10 9 8 7 6 5 4 3 2 1
Printed and bound in China

ABRAMS
THE ART OF BOOKS SINCE 1949

115 West 18th Street
New York, NY 10011
www.abramsbooks.com

CONTENTS

INTRODUCTION

Don'ts for Wives, 1913 "So many women exhaust their artistic power in getting married, which is, after all, a comparatively easy business. It takes a perfect artist to remain married—married in the perfect sense of the term; but most of us have to be content to muddle through."

Weddings can be among the most defining and memorable events of our lives. They conjure anticipation, excitement, anxiety, romance, solemnity, trepidation, and, indeed, any combination of these emotions. A wedding allows the bride and groom to indulge their imaginations—and make public and lasting their commitment to one another—in a manner and style befitting their personal tastes and preferences. For some this could be realizing a childhood dream of a fairy-tale wedding, while for others it might be arranging a small gathering of close friends and family with the least possible fuss. No matter how simple, weddings entail thought and planning, and they usually involve a substantial financial outlay. They can also prove overwhelming in practical matters of dress, decoration, catering, and venue.

But perhaps the most compelling visual element of a wedding is the bride; whether intentionally or not, most attention will fall on her. Even the most nonchalant bride will find it difficult to escape an expectation to cultivate an arresting impression of beauty and style.

A to Z of Wedding Style is intended as an informative, though lighthearted, resource on wedding styles past and present. It functions as a visual vocabulary of wedding styles as they relate to fashion (for example, dress and accessories, fabrics and silhouettes), the wedding party (the best man and bridesmaids), articles associated with weddings (champagne and trousseau), and sentiments reflective of the occasion. The book does not aim to provide an exhaustive commentary; neither does it address the subject of faith. Instead it presents, in encyclopedic format, a compendium of facts, quotes, and anecdotes concerning the prevailing styles and traditions that have influenced celebrations of marriage in Western society.

HOW TO USE THIS BOOK

Although *A to Z of Wedding Style* provides a point of reference for modern brides-to-be, it intends to inform, inspire, and amuse a wide audience interested in the subject of weddings and wedding style.

The quotations have been selected from a variety of sources, from the nineteenth century to the present day.

For further information, the reference section starting on page 139 is organized by source and provides all the relevant page numbers for entries in *A to Z of Wedding Style*.

We hope that *A to Z of Wedding Style* will prove a useful and inspirational resource for brides-to-be and anyone interested in the subject of weddings.

A is for ACCESSORIES

A-LINE

The A-line refers to the form of a dress or skirt that is narrower, or fitted, at the hips and flares gently wider toward the hem. A common shape for skirts and dresses in the 1950s, the A-line remains a popular choice for bridal gowns, as it flatters most figures (and is effective at concealing pear-shaped silhouettes). An enduring favorite, the A-line connotes refinement and a love of form.

ACCESSORIES

Small objects of adornment or articles of clothing worn to complete or complement an outfit, such as jewelry, bags, or scarves.

Jenny Packham (b.1965), British fashion designer and Bridal Buyer's Bridal Designer of the Year, 2011 and 2012

"Brides love a complete look on their wedding day."

Christian Dior (1905–57), French fashion designer

"The less you can afford for your frocks, the more care you must take with your accessories."

Bags

Receptacles carried in the hand or on the shoulder used for storing personal items, such as a purse, diary, stationery, cosmetic products—and, in modern society—a cell phone and keys. Bags are often selected for their specific decorative qualities to complete an outfit. The carrying of handbags was established in the eighteenth century, prior to which decorative fabric pockets containing personal items were worn at the waist.

Bags come in a wide variety of shapes, sizes, and styles, including baguette, barrel, clutch, shoulder, satchel, and tote, and they are manufactured in a wide range of materials, colors, and finishes. Bags now form part of a lucrative global market, with luxury bags accounting for a significant proportion of designer sales. Hermès was the first designer brand to name particular styles of their bags after actresses and celebrities—the Birkin bag, named after Jane Birkin, and the Kelly bag, named after Grace Kelly, being the most famous. This practice remains popular among contemporary designers.

Not all brides choose to carry a handbag on their wedding day. Sometimes it is not deemed compatible with the dress or the look they have selected; sometimes they already have other handheld accoutrements to consider, such as a bouquet. Often it falls upon the maid of honor to look after, and keep close at hand, the personal items a bride might require.

Gloves

Gloves represent another article of personal adornment valued for both their practical and decorative qualities. Historically, gloves offered a protective covering for the hands with separate sheaths for each finger and thumb that shielded the skin against cold, heat, and harmful substances. During the medieval period, however, women started to wear linen and silk gloves as an ornament of fashion. From Elizabethan times, the upper classes began to wear richly embroidered gloves as symbols of wealth, status, delicacy, and grace. In the 1940s and 1950s it was still considered appropriate for women to wear gloves when in town or attending social occasions such as weddings. Gloves made of fine materials, such as kid leather, silk, or lace, have maintained their association with elegance and are still worn by some women for formal occasions. Traditionally, the length of the glove along the forearm is determined by the formality of the occasion at which it is worn. Gloves worn for formal wear come in three lengths: wrist; elbow; and opera, or full-length, which extend beyond the elbow.

The Etiquette of Marriage, 1857

"The trembling bride with inward joy
Pulls off the left-hand glove,
That on her finger may be put
The pledge of mutual love."

Handkerchief

A small square of fabric, usually linen, cotton, or silk. Men's handkerchiefs tend to be plain or printed and are typically worn in the breast pocket of a suit jacket as decorative accessories. A woman's handkerchief might be decorated with embroidery or a lace border. Handkerchiefs are a wise consideration for wedding guests prone to shedding a tear.

Hats

Some brides prefer to wear a hat instead of a veil (and hats might be thought of as a more pragmatic choice, as they can be worn again). It is customary for the mothers of the bride and groom to wear a hat that complements their outfit.

Increasingly, women do not remove their hats when indoors, as they are thought to constitute part of their outfit. Men, on the other hand, should always remove their hats when inside. The mother of the bride dictates when others should remove their hats at a wedding; until she removes hers, others are expected to keep theirs on.

Stephen Jones (b.1957), British milliner

"Back in the day you would often have a specific hairstyle to go with a hat. Your hat would only be a specific accent in your over-all look, and hairstyle, make-up, and outfit would all be co-ordinated. Make sure you don't just wear an outfit and a hat, but that your hat is part of your outfit."

Philip Treacy (b.1967), Irish milliner

"The success of a hat definitely lies with balancing the personality of the wearer with the type of occasion. . . . Don't listen to those rules about face shape. Try on 100 different hats if you can, until you find the one that suits you best. It's a trial and error thing."

Alison Adburgham (b.1912), British journalist and fashion historian

"Hats are the dragonflies of the dress world."

ALTERNATIVE

A wedding dress is not the only choice; Camilla Parker Bowles chose to wear a floor-length coat by Robinson Valentine over her gown for her wedding to Prince Charles in 2005. When Sophia Loren was married for the second time in 1966 to Carlo Ponti Sr., she dispensed with all the traditional bridal accoutrements—gown, bouquet, and veil—and selected a wool coat for her wedding.

Brides marrying in exotic locations can even choose to say "I do" in a bridal T-shirt. In the early 1990s, bridal wear designer Ronald Joyce designed an oversized T-shirt printed with the words "The Bride" on the front and "Just Married" on the back.

B *is for* BRIDESMAIDS

"*Their gowns should be as dainty and pretty as you can devise, but they should be, of course, of a less handsome and striking material than your own gown.*"
Etiquette for Women, 1919

BANNS

From Middle English, meaning "proclamation," the "banns" refer to the public announcement of an intended marriage, given in church, in order that any persons who know of an impediment to the union might have the opportunity to make an objection.

BEAUTY

Vogue, April 1920

"For the bride nothing is too rare or beautiful."

Harper's Bazaar, May 1952

"A bride is beautiful by tradition. In a moment of apotheosis, she floats down the aisle, [as] immaculate and cool as the swan princess."

Vogue, April 1940

"Beauty is a secret. Keep it so. The average young male finds the fabrication of beauty either ludicrous and distasteful, or demeaning. Never let him see you doing ridiculous-looking exercises or in a masque. Never tell him you have a broken fingernail or gained four pounds, or can't do a thing with your hair. Reserve these woes for your female companions who will understand."

BEST MAN

The best man is traditionally the principal male attendant of the groom in the wedding ceremony. He is usually a close friend or relative. The best man is responsible for ensuring that the groom arrives at the wedding venue in plenty of time, and he also safeguards the rings until they are required. It is conventional for the best man to give a speech and toast the newlyweds.

Wedding Etiquette, 1966

"The best man should be unmarried, someone with an aptitude for looking after details, and a man who will not be easily flustered. The cheery man who can rise to any occasion and get things done is welcome."

Vera Wang (b.1949), American bridal wear designer

"Although the best man has a unique role in the proceedings, stylistically there should be little to differentiate him from the rest of the groomsmen; uniformity is the goal."

BIAS CUT

The technique of cutting fabric on the diagonal, credited to the Parisian couturier Madeleine Vionnet (1876–1975). Cutting fabric on the bias utilizes the natural stretch in the diagonal qualities of the cloth. As a result, the fabric emphasizes the natural lines and curves of the body and allows it to drape softly and gracefully. Cutting on the bias also allows for an unbroken line, which removes the need for seams that can draw attention to certain areas of the body, such as the stomach. The bias cut is thus considered a highly sensual, flattering cut. It is associated with the soft crêpe and slinky satin gowns worn by 1930s Hollywood stars.

Madeleine Vionnet (1876–1975), French couturier

"The dress must not hang on the body but follow its lines. It must accompany its wearer and when a woman smiles, the dress must smile with her."

Roland Mouret (b.1961), French fashion designer

"The bias cut turns the fabric to water. It allows the fabric to speak."

BLUSHER

A section of veil that covers the bride's face as she walks down the aisle. The blusher can be worn during the entire ceremony (until the first kiss), or it can be pulled back over the bride's face before the

father of the bride gives his daughter away. Some
religious institutions require a bride to show her
face during the ceremony.

BODICE
An article of female dress that covers the body from
the neck to the waist, the bodice was also a specific
type of garment worn by women in Europe between
1700 and 1900. The term also refers to the upper
portion of a dress, as distinguished from the skirt
and sleeves. To ensure a comfortable and flattering
fit, bodices should be tailored to the torso.

BOUQUET
Brides have carried some form of bouquet since the
earliest times. In Ancient Greece and Rome, grains
were carried as a symbol of fertility. In the medieval
and early modern eras, herbs were incorporated,
owing to their medicinal qualities and a belief that
they might ward off evil spirits and safeguard the
bride and her future happiness.

The most popular shapes for bouquets are the
teardrop-shaped cascade and the waterfall. These
are elaborate formations and require a professional
florist skilled in the art of wiring flowers. Many
brides, however, favor smaller posies or simple,
hand-tied bunches held together with a length of
ribbon. These are easier to achieve, and the artistic
bride may feel comfortable making one herself.
Pageants are also a popular modern choice and take
the form of long-stemmed flowers cradled in the
bride's arm.

Vogue, February 1930   "As the blushing bride floats down the aisle, she
carries in her trembling hand the bouquet sent to
her by the nervous gentleman who awaits her in the

chancel. If she is a wise little bride, she has ordered the bouquet herself. This, *Vogue* finds, is loveliest when made of lilies-of-the-valley and white orchids, or lilies-of-the-valley and fragrant orange or citron blossoms."

Harper's Bazaar, March 1958   "Most romantic, most delicious of all—the fragile bunch of freesias and lilies-of-the-valley."

Vogue, May 1916   "A bride who elects a country wedding may carry a bit of sunshine in her bouquet. We suggest this bouquet, a yellow sunburst shading from a cream centre of freesia down through snapdragon, yellow daisies, and [Mrs.] Aaron Ward roses, ending in a blaze of marigold. Acacia weights the ribbon."

Vogue, February 1930   "*Vogue* cautions the bride to give the florist a sample of the satin from her dress, as there are many different tones of white satin ribbon."

The Complete Guide to Wedding Etiquette, 1960   "Beautiful flowers can be ruined by a bad florist, whereas inexpensive flowers can be made into a fine bouquet by a good one."

BOUTONNIERE

Vogue, May 1916   A single flower, or spray of flowers, worn in a jacket's buttonhole. It is customary at weddings for the groom, best man, ushers, and father of the bride to wear a boutonniere, which is more commonly referred to as a "buttonhole."

Vogue, October 1936   "Gardenias, roses, or lilies-of-the-valley are usually worn by the men in the wedding party, with gardenias as current favourites. The bridegroom's, or the groom's and best man's, may differ from those of the usher, but all should be white."

BRIDAL BOUTIQUE

A specialty shop dedicated to the sale of bridal wear and accessories, which stocks a wide variety of off-the-rack gowns by a variety of designers and manufacturers. The gowns are ready-made and will be altered as necessary by the boutique. Many department stores have in-house bridal boutiques.

Advertisement for Harrods Bridal Boutique in *Brides Magazine*, Summer 1962 "For the day that will live in your memory entrust all the details of your wedding to Harrods. . . . The outfits of your bridesmaids and attendants will be perfectly partnered to yours. Then, wearing a truly spellbinding gown chosen from the Trousseau Room, you can enjoy the most wonderful day of your life."

BRIDESMAIDS

Attendants of the bride who assist with wedding preparations, as required, and on the day in helping the bride with her attire. There is no prescribed number of bridesmaids a bride might have, although many tend to select a couple of close friends and have younger relatives, or the children of close friends, as flower girls. Increasingly, as people get married later in life, bridesmaids are no longer exclusively young or unmarried. Although bridesmaids are expected to complement the bride, they should not overshadow her and are, to all intents and purposes, pretty accessories.

Vogue, April 1920 "The perfection of a perfect wedding also concerns the bridesmaids. Theirs must be the part to look charming, yet not too charming; distinctive, yet not too prominent—a subtle role to play."

Marianne Ostier (1902–76), American jewelry designer "The bridesmaids should recognize that they are present to provide a beautiful frame for a beautiful picture."

Etiquette for Women, 1919   "Their gowns should be as dainty and pretty as you can devise, but they should be, of course, of a less handsome and striking material than your own gown."

Lady Behave: A Guide to Modern Manners, 1956   "Since the bride usually chooses the dresses, she naturally picks colours and styles that will make a good background for her."

Vogue, May 1916   "A bride must be absolutely assured of her own loveliness before she permits her bridesmaid to wear anything half so charming as this. It is of silver embroidered rose faille interspersed with bands of rose tulle, and plump little faille roses blossom all over it. Silver lace edges it, and a blue ribbon forms both girdle and the note of contrast."

"BRIDEZILLA"

The term "Bridezilla" first came into common parlance in the early twenty-first century and refers to brides who are particularly obsessive or overbearing about their wedding day and controlling and demanding of the other parties involved (usually the groom, bridesmaids, or mother of the bride). Bridezillas have fixed ideas about how their wedding should be and are typically petulant and unwilling to compromise. In recent years the television documentary *Bridezillas* has given further attention to brides-to-be of this ilk, highlighting characteristics such as the tendency to force bridesmaids to undergo strict weight loss prior to the wedding.

BUDGET

Vogue, May 1918   "This bride didn't need to spend a fortune on her veil, since a little real lace is often more effective than a great deal."

In March 2014 CNN quoted the average cost of a US wedding ceremony at $30,000, up from $7,800 in 1984.

The substantial cost of weddings has forced many couples to be particularly savvy, especially with their choice of wedding attire. Thrift shops and online auction sites such as eBay provide the modern bride—and groom—with affordable options for wedding attire and can be good alternatives for picking up a vintage bargain.

The global recession that followed the banking crisis of 2008 prompted many clothing stores to respond to the need for more affordable bridal attire. In January 2009, British Home Stores (BHS) retailed a simple white bridal ensemble with shoes for £100 ($170).

Savings can also be made in other areas, such as with simple printed invitations produced on a home computer and making use of shoes and other accessories already owned by the bride and her friends. Thinking of elegant alternatives—candles instead of fresh flowers for table decorations, for example—can also reduce costs substantially. There is an abundance of blogs and online forums providing instruction and inspiration for those wishing to keep costs under control and put into practice their own creative skills.

Simply staying away from products advertised with the word "wedding" can make things a lot more affordable. Dance shoes, for example, offer an alternative to traditional wedding shoes—and are not dissimilar to many of the styles available in bridal boutiques.

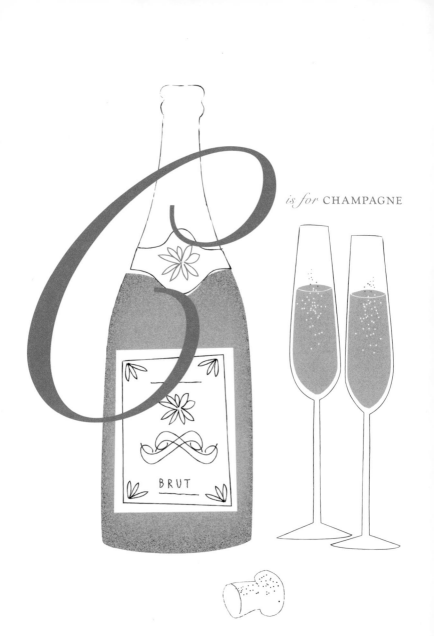

is for CHAMPAGNE

BRUT

CAKE

In early times, a wedding cake bore a closer approximation to bread than a sweet cake, and it was filled with grains as a symbol of fertility. As trade routes expanded in the sixteenth century, spices and preserved fruits were added to recipes, and the wedding cake increasingly began to resemble the modern fruitcake. Wedding cakes became more elaborate during the nineteenth century, when cakes with several tiers decorated with intricate icing and spun sugar gained popularity. It was at this time that the association between the wedding cake and the bride's wedding dress became established.

Today couples are faced with a range of confections from which to choose. Individual frosted cupcakes arranged in tiers have also enjoyed popularity in the early twenty-first century.

The cutting of the wedding cake can be thought of as the first task the married couple undertakes together, and the custom of the bride and groom feeding each other the first slice endures as a romantic tradition. The amount of cake the bride gives to her groom symbolizes the size of her love for him, while the amount of icing the groom leaves on his wife's lips is indicative of the sweetness of the life he will offer her.

Some couples keep the tradition of freezing the top tier of a wedding cake and saving it for their first wedding anniversary.

The Complete Guide to
Wedding Etiquette, 1960

"The cake is sometimes cut with a saw provided for that purpose, and as this is rather a hard task, the icing being difficult to cut through, it is generally considered sufficient if the bride makes [only] the first incision."

CASUAL

Bridal ensembles do not have to be formal or flamboyant. When artist Yoko Ono wed Beatle John Lennon in Gibraltar in 1969, she chose to wear a white minidress and kneesocks.

CHAMPAGNE

Champagne is the traditional drink for toasting the bride and groom at the wedding reception. Champagne's association with French culture, its position as a premium drink, and its effervescent qualities all connote luxury and situate it as "perfect" for a special occasion. The cost of champagne can, however, be off-putting. Unless the couple are connoisseurs, there are many good alternatives.

Vogue, April 1941

"[Here's t]o you . . . if you are ingenious enough . . . to substitute for the traditional champagne, tall glasses of white wine, soda, ice and mint; or a punch made with domestic champagne."

"The choice of champagne itself involves a wide range in price, but not necessarily in quality. While a vintage champagne will be expensive, a good non-vintage variety, French or domestic, might be better than some poor vintage years, and at a considerably lower price."

Vogue, July 1958

"It is best not to ice more than is needed, since the wine is less good when chilled a second time."

CIVIL CEREMONY

A nonreligious marriage ceremony performed by a legal registrar or justice of the peace is commonly referred to as a "civil ceremony." Although many couples who do not regularly attend places of worship still wish to marry in a church or other religious institution, the decline in religiosity in Western culture has led to an increase in civil wedding services.

CIVIL PARTNERSHIP

A state-sanctioned union between couples of the same sex that affords many of the same legal and financial rights enjoyed by married heterosexual couples. The first civil unions in the US were offered by the state of Vermont in 2000.

British singer Elton John and his long-term partner David Furnish were among the first celebrity gay couples to take advantage of the new legislation. Both wore dark morning suits that set a standard of dress for traditional-style civil partnership ceremonies. Other popular choices for wedding attire among gay men are patterned fabrics, harmonizing suits in either light or bright colors, or more casual outfits that reflect the wearers' individual identities.

The choices made by lesbian couples for their wedding day are equally varied. Although the "classic white dress" is traditionally associated with a heterosexual bride, many gay women choose to wear white for their weddings. However, it is unusual for both women to wear a white dress. When American television personality Ellen DeGeneres married actress Portia de Rossi in California in 2008, she wore a loose-fitting ensemble of white trousers, white shirt, and white waistcoat; de Rossi wore a long white halter-neck gown. Other couples have married in colorful dresses or suits. Just as for all marriages, there is no prescribed formula.

COLOR

Vogue, June 2008 "The white gown is forever classic, but a coloured one is a modern standout."

Although a white wedding gown persists as an ideal to which many brides aspire, bridal wear does not have to be exclusively white. While many women do not feel it appropriate to fulfill the traditional stereotype of the innocent, virgin bride on their wedding day, others simply do not like wearing white or prefer to choose a gown that they have more chance of wearing again. The vogue for selecting a colored gown is not new. The Romans considered yellow to be the most auspicious color in which to wed, as they associated the hue with Hymen, goddess of marriage and fertility. Throughout the early modern period, brides belonging to the elite classes tended to marry in silk robes of rich colors. By the eighteenth century, silver and gold were incorporated into bridal gowns for the prosperous, and patterned silks in yellows and blues were popular, too. It was not until 1840 that white became established as the norm for wedding dresses, a development in large part a consequence of Queen Victoria's decision to select white for her marriage to Prince Albert of Saxe-Coburg and Gotha in February 1840.

A survey undertaken by the *Daily Mail* revealed that only half of brides in the period 2000–10 wore a white dress. Actress Julianne Moore opted for a lilac sheath dress by Italian fashion label Prada, which she accessorized with a chartreuse bag and shoes, for her 2003 wedding to Bart Freundlich. Elizabeth Taylor experimented with a few bridal looks over her eight marriages. For her fourth wedding, to Eddie Fisher, in 1959, the actress selected a green hooded gown reminiscent of the popular medieval folklore character Maid Marian. Wallis Simpson broke with tradition when she married Prince Edward in 1937 by wearing a simple, high-necked, long-sleeved gown by American couturier Mainbocher (1890–1976) in "Wallis blue."

Burlesque performer Dita Von Teese married singer Marilyn Manson in a Gold Label gown of deep purple shot taffeta by British fashion designer Dame Vivienne Westwood (b.1941). The dress bore all the hallmarks of Westwood's style, including a built-in corset and billowing full skirt.

Vera Wang (b.1949), American bridal wear designer

"Color creates an ambience, and is often a mechanism for uniting elements of a wedding into a cohesive scheme."

Color can be incorporated into the bridal scheme in more subtle ways than the gown itself; it can provide a small, yet noticeable, point of contrast to a traditional white gown. This could take the form of brightly colored accessories; for example, shoes, brooches, and flowers, or trimmings such as bows and ribbons.

COMPROMISE
So much attention is focused on how the bride looks on her wedding day that sometimes the groom can appear to be something of a supporting actor in the proceedings. Although expected to look his smartest, in reality the groom's outfit is often unmemorable. It is not uncommon for brides to become so completely absorbed in planning and realizing their particular vision for their wedding day that the groom's opinions and preferences may be overlooked or rejected. Marriage is a partnership that entails compromise and consultation, and these qualities can form the basis of wedding planning, too.

| *Wedding Etiquette*, 1966 | "Don't imagine [that] your point of view is the only one." |

| Raquel Welch (b.1940), American actress | "We all have a childhood dream that when there is love, everything goes like silk, but the reality is that marriage requires a lot of compromise." |

CONFETTI

Of Italian origin, *confetti* was the term first used to describe the sweets given to guests as a memento of the wedding. Now confetti has come to mean the small decorative pieces of paper, flower petals, or rice that are thrown over the bride and groom after the ceremony. The custom of showering newlyweds with tokens of good luck stems back to Ancient Greece and Rome, when grain was used, encouraging fertility where it fell.

COORDINATION

| *Vogue*, April 1924 | "A large bridal party is necessarily spectacular and is most effective when it adheres to a definite period and a coherent colour scheme." |

CORSAGE

From the French, meaning "bodice," a corsage is a bouquet of real or artificial flowers worn at the neck, shoulder, or wrist. Corsages are often worn by the mothers of the bride and groom. It is also becoming popular for bridesmaids to wear corsages rather than to carry bouquets, as they are often cheaper than posies created by florists and leave bridesmaids with hands free to help the bride with tasks such as arranging her bridal train or scattering petals in front of her as she walks up the aisle.

CORSET

A close-fitting undergarment, traditionally stiffened

with whalebone and fastened with lacings, which gives shape and support.

The body-conscious fashions of the 1980s gave way to a trend for wearing undergarments as outerwear. British fashion designer Dame Vivienne Westwood (b.1941) introduced corsets as outerwear in her fashion collection for Spring/Summer 1985. The style was a popular bridal wear choice in the 1990s.

CRAVAT

Potentially an important wedding accessory for the groom and groomsmen, a cravat is a form of necktie that originated in seventeenth-century Croatia as a forerunner to the modern tie and bow tie. Cravats are loose pieces of fabric tied around the neck and often secured to a dress shirt with a pin. They can be narrow or wide and of plain or patterned silk or cotton, depending on the formality of the occasion. There are numerous styles and methods for tying a cravat, with the "ascot" being among the most popular for formal occasions.

CRINOLINE

Derived from the French *crin*, meaning "coarse hair," originally "crinoline" referred to fabric woven from horsehair or linen that was used to stiffen or add volume to the petticoats necessary for creating a full-skirted silhouette. By 1856 the term also was used to describe the lightweight, cagelike structure that hung from a woman's waist as a series of graduated hoops to achieve the same outline without layers of encumbering petticoats. The crinoline was an important feature of mid-nineteenth-century wedding dress that supported the fashionable silhouette. Modern brides who favor this outline can achieve the same effect with an underskirt made of tulle.

is for DRESS

DANCING SHOES

Although many brides have plenty of experience in wearing towering stilettos, the chances of being comfortable in high heels for an entire day and evening are marginal. Many brides, therefore, select an additional pair of comfortable shoes for once the formalities are over in which to enjoy their night of dancing with their guests at the reception. Flats and pumps are popular choices, but there are plenty of options for those who still want to make a style statement: customized Converse trainers decorated with ribbons, Swarovski crystals, or embroidered details including the couple's names and wedding date have emerged as modern favorites.

DESIGNER BRIDES

The cost of purchasing or commissioning a gown by an internationally renowned designer is prohibitive for the majority of brides. The cachet of designer fashions does, however, lend itself to the wedding gown—which many brides consider to be the most significant dress they will ever wear—and so some brides choose to indulge. Most still will only be able to afford off-the-rack creations from designers with specialty bridal ranges. Couture creations generally cost upward of $50,000, but for those for whom money is not an issue, the allure of commissioning a designer to create a gown to their individual requirements can represent the ultimate bridal fantasy.

Reem Acra, Lebanese-American fashion and bridal wear designer

"For me, to make her dream come true, by creating her wedding dress for her, is a gift! And it's an opportunity for me, as well; she's laying all of her hopes and dreams in my hands. It's very exciting for me, too, as a designer."

DIAMONDS

Marianne Ostier (1902–76), American jewelry designer

"Supreme in the human imagination is the diamond, the hardest of all stones. The word 'diamond' captures this significance, for it is from the Greek *adamas*, meaning 'unconquerable, the tameless.'"

Elizabeth Arden advertisement in *Brides Magazine*, Spring 1962

"Diamonds sparkle, but the brightest way to shine is with those jewels of nature—your own eyes."

DIET

Many brides-to-be embark on some form of diet and exercise regimen before their wedding. Planning the day can be extremely stressful, and many women naturally lose weight in the immediate run-up to the ceremony. While there is nothing wrong with dieting to help you feel your best, it is, of course, ill advised to take it to extremes. It is unlikely that the groom and guests will wish to see a bride transformed beyond all recognition.

Elsa Schiaparelli (1890–1973), Italian fashion designer

"Never fit a dress to the body, but train a body to fit the dress."

DRESS

Some brides-to-be tend to have a firm idea about the type of dress that they envision wearing on their wedding day; others have never given it a thought before they get engaged. Regardless, finding "the dress," or at least a dress that is cherished enough to be selected, should be fun, enjoyable, and even a time for experimentation. Long versus short, full versus columnar, plain versus embellished, strapless versus sleeved, minimal versus extravagant, avant-garde versus traditional—there really is something to express all tastes and personalities. A wedding gown can also comprise a bricolage of various styles and design features. The key is finding a design that both suits the personality of the bride and draws attention to the physical features she wants to emphasize most.

Vera Wang (b.1949), American bridal wear designer	"For most women a wedding gown represents far more than just a dress. It is also the embodiment of a dream, perhaps one she has nurtured since childhood. In this fantasy of idealized happiness, the groom represents perfection and the face of all human possibility. The instant a woman becomes engaged, however, all that energy and passion gets transferred to her dress. What follows can be something akin to madness."
Alexandra Wentworth (b.1965), American actress	"My concern was never 'Is he the one?' but 'What the hell am I going to wear?'"
Vogue, May 1916	"Mercifully vanished are those days when one promised to obey in a stiff, high, long concoction of unbecomingness. Now the wedding gown is just a shade less charming than the bride."
Vogue, April 1925	"The wedding gown and each detail of the trousseau should be not merely 'bridal' but suited to the bride who wears them."
Justine Picardie (b.1961), editor of *Harper's Bazaar*	"There has to be a first dress, like a first kiss; there has to be."
Christian Dior (1905–57), French couturier	"A dress is a fleeting architecture designed to ennoble the feminine body's proportions."
Coco Chanel (1883–1971), French couturier	"Fashion is at once both caterpillar and butterfly. . . . There must be dresses that crawl and dresses that fly."
Norma Shearer (1902–83), American actress	"The right dress can triumph over any situation, build any mood, create any illusion, and make any woman into the sort of person she most desires to be."

is for ENGAGEMENT RING

"*Choosing the right engagement ring inspires almost as much trembling among grooms-to-be as the proposal itself.*"
Vogue, March 2004

ELEGANCE

Elegance is the sartorial standard most brides strive to achieve on their wedding day. Intrinsically associated with personal style, elegance is an instinctive sense of being that relates to the way in which a woman moves and behaves (deportment and demeanor) and the stylistic choices she makes (taste and style). True elegance is innate; it can be refined but never cultivated or affected. Most important, elegance is timeless and transcends fashion, class, and wealth. A humbly budgeted bride may therefore be eminently elegant, while the richest society bride equally could appear garish and vulgar.

Christian Dior (1905–57), French couturier	"Elegance must be the right combination of distinction, naturalness, care, and simplicity. Outside this, believe me, there is no elegance. Only pretension."
Diana Vreeland (1903–89), British curator, and editor of *Harper's Bazaar* and *Vogue*	"Fashion is a passing thing—a thing of fancy, fantasy and feeling. Elegance is innate."
Yves Saint Laurent (1936–2008), French fashion designer	"Elegance is a dress too stunning to dare to wear it twice."
Editorial on the wedding of Miss Felicity D'Abreu, *Harper's Bazaar*, February 1960	"This is the way we like a bride to look: serene, confident, adding something of her own to the picture cast by fashion and tradition."
Genevieve Antoine Dariaux (b.1914), French author on etiquette	"A long, formal wedding dress is elegant only when it is utterly simple, even somewhat austere."
Vera Wang (b.1949), American bridal wear designer	"It requires enormous confidence and style to wear white elegantly and effectively."
Franco Moschino (1950–94), Italian fashion designer	"If you can't be elegant, at least be extravagant!"

EMANUELS (THE)

David and Elizabeth Emanuel are British fashion designers who created Lady Diana Spencer's wedding dress for her marriage to the Prince of Wales in July 1981.

The Emanuels were introduced to Lady Diana Spencer for the first time in February 1981; just one month later they were asked to create what has become an iconic dress. The design was a gown of ivory silk taffeta with a 25-foot (7.6-m) train. It was adorned with antique lace and decorative details that included flounces, taffeta bows, and embroidery incorporating thousands of pearls and sequins. It was heralded as the quintessential fairy-tale wedding gown.

David (b.1952) and Elizabeth (b.1953) Emanuel, British fashion designers

"Wedding dresses in that period had tended to be quite starchy and formal—very traditional, A-line, and made of white satin. There was no real magic or sense of fairy tale, and that was what we wanted to create. The fact [that] we made the dress in ivory was different, too, and started a whole trend in nonwhite wedding dresses, not only in ivory but also in other shades.

"We wanted Diana to look like no princess has ever looked before. So we set out to discover the length of the longest royal wedding dress train. Eventually we discovered that one royal bride had had a 7-metre [23-foot] train. We joked with Diana that we could go one better—in fact, two feet better—and create a 7.6-metre [25-foot] train. She loved the idea and laughed."

Elizabeth Emanuel (b.1953), British fashion designer

"It was designed really just to catch the light, not so that you would actually see the sequins in the veil, but so that it would twinkle and look magical under the lights."

EMBROIDERY

Decorative needlework, undertaken by hand or machine, using thread and needle to stitch into fabric; beads, pearls, sequins, and other decorative items can be embroidered onto fabrics to embellish them by adding texture, shine, and color.

"Appliqué" refers to a specific style of embroidery used on fabric, lace, and other materials, such as leather, in which cutout motifs are applied to another surface.

ENGAGEMENT RING

Vogue, February 1930
"The engagement ring is most acceptable when it is a flawless diamond solitaire, simply set, emerald cut, and preferably large!"

Marianne Ostier (1902–76), American jewelry designer
"The ring calls attention to the hand. It invites the gaze, which, while admiring the ring, is also aware of the fingers that are the background to the jewel."

"The diamond may be brilliant cut; this is conservative but in impeccable taste. It should be set in thin, high prongs of the chosen metal, so as to give the fullest play to the light from all its facets and to take full effect from all its irradiating brilliance."

Engagement rings tend to be much showier than wedding bands, as they incorporate precious stones. The solitaire diamond set in a band of gold or platinum is now a popular choice, but while diamonds were set in engagement bands as early as the fourth century, they did not become the stone of choice for another thousand years.

Some brides-to-be wish to break with tradition and to select something that better suits their personalities and stylistic preferences. Brightly colored stones such as rubies and oversize pearls are becoming increasingly popular.

Traditionally a groom is supposed to spend the equivalent of one month's salary on the engagement ring, although many now consider this an outdated custom. It also used to be considered a good omen to include the fiancé's birthstone in an engagement ring, although again, this is no longer common practice. Birthstones vary across cultures, but the widely accepted ones for Britain and North America are:

Month	Stone	Symbolic meaning
January	Garnet	Truth and constancy
February	Amethyst	Sincerity
March	Bloodstone and aquamarine	Courage and justice
April	Diamond	Innocence and purity
May	Emerald	Hope
June	Agate and pearl	Protection (agate); purity and innocence (pearls)
July	Ruby	Passion
August	Sardonyx and peridot	Fertility and conjugal happiness (sardonyx); felicity and protection (peridot)
September	Sapphire	Faithfulness, sincerity and truth
October	Opal and tourmaline	Fidelity and assurance (opal); balance and protection (tourmaline)
November	Topaz	Cheerfulness
December	Turquoise	Unselfishness

Carat, clarity, cut, and color are important considerations when selecting a diamond engagement ring. Carat is a measure of weight; the higher the carat, the larger the diamond. The clarity rating of a diamond is determined by the number of flaws and inclusions in the stone. The scale ranges from "flawless" to "most desirable" to "imperfect"; the fewer the flaws, the greater the quality and value.

The cut of the diamond has an impact on its brilliance. The more facets (surfaces) there are, the more it will sparkle. Color is rated according to a scale that runs from "D," the highest, to "Z," the lowest. Subtle tones of brown or yellow are undesirable and must not be mistaken for fancy colored diamonds, which are extremely rare.

ETHEREAL

Vogue, September 2011 (on Kate Moss's wedding)

"Like Pre-Raphaelite visions in diaphanous silk and delicate eyelet petticoat dresses, angelic flower girls and bridesmaids (and a page boy) encircle the bride."

ETHICAL

Growing concerns in the 1980s and 1990s regarding the environment and issues of sustainability made their presence felt in the arena of bridal wear. In 1996, Hessnatur Textilien, a German mail-order company specializing in eco-friendly clothing, celebrated its tenth anniversary by establishing a wedding-dress loan scheme of designs made from sustainable materials such as undyed hemp and silk. The company sought to tackle the wasteful aspect of "one-time" wedding dresses by recycling them among several brides.

The notion of recycling wedding dresses is not new and extends back to the wedding-dress rental services established during World War II to tackle the problems of wartime shortages.

Mining metals and precious stones can be environmentally harmful, and the labor force can be subjected to unfair wages and dangerous working conditions. In response, some jewelers now specialize in ethically sourced precious metals and stones. Jewelers should be able to advise on the provenance of the metals and stones used for the jewelry they sell, but companies including Brilliant Earth, CRED Jewellery, and Ingle & Rhode are among those who offer ethical assurances.

is for FASCINATOR

FABRIC

Harper's Bazaar, March 1958 "The sum of lace and satin is a wonderful wedding dress—and pounds well spent."

The fabric chosen for a gown is instrumental in creating a pleasing aesthetic and image, offering variety and nuance in color, tone, texture, weight, and decorative effect. Not all fabrics are suitable for all styles of gowns, as they behave and drape in different ways. Whereas structured fabrics, such as duchess satin, possess body and lend themselves to conventional weddings gowns, soft fabrics, including silk crêpes and chiffons, drape beautifully and are suited to the seductive, looser-fitting styles that skim the body.

Brocade
A rich, decorative, woven fabric often made with colored silks and gold and silver threads. Owing to the elaborate ornamentation and the weight of the fabric, it is best suited to formal gowns or for designs intending to capture a sense of historic grandeur.

Charmeuse
A soft, lightweight, and luxurious satin fabric with a subdued luster. Charmeuse is considered to be a glamorous fabric that looks especially beautiful when draped over the body. Many of the seductive gowns worn by Hollywood stars in the 1930s were crafted of charmeuse. Owing to its shine, it is best left unembellished.

Chiffon
A soft, delicately sheer fabric in plain weave of silk or rayon with a soft, or sometimes stiff, finish. Chiffon is often used in double layers and for dresses, scarves, and veils. Its transparency means that it requires a lining if used for a dress or gown.

Crêpe
A light, gauzy fabric, usually of silk or cotton, with a crinkled surface. Crêpes are extremely versatile and can be draped and embellished or tailored and left plain. They are perfect for capturing an air of understated elegance.

Crêpe de Chine ·	A fine-quality silk material, lustrous and slightly crinkled.
Duchess satin	A substantial, luxurious satin, usually of silk, which has a high thread count and is shiny on one side.
Faille	An untwilled, slightly glossy silk fabric. Failles are sometimes stiff but are usually limp with a good draping quality.
Georgette	A sheer, sensuous fabric constructed from a strong crêpe of fibers, woven from hard, twisted yarns to produce a dull, pebbly surface. Georgette fabric requires a lining.
Lamé	A textile woven with a weft of metallic thread.
Moiré	A silk or synthetic silk impressed with a wavy or watered pattern that is created by passing the textile between rollers engraved with the design.
Nylon	A synthetic, silky material intended as a man-made substitute for natural silk. First used commercially in 1938 to produce toothbrush bristles, nylon quickly became the material of choice for women's stockings and as a cheaper substitute for natural fabrics.
Vogue, April 1952	"Nylon being the consistent daily magic that it is in today's world."
Organdie	A thin, plain-weave cotton fabric with a stiff finish.
Organza	A sheer, fine, and crisp silk fabric used in several layers for diaphanous gowns.
Peau de soie	A soft, heavy, grosgrain silk, closely woven and with a dull satin face on both sides.
Satin	A fabric with a smooth, glossy finish. Satin has presence and looks luxurious either plain or embellished. It possesses the weight and body necessary for a full, gathered skirt, A-line style, or a structured bustier.
Shot silk	A silk with different colored warp and weft thread that results in the surface color changing with light or movement.
Silk	A natural fiber with an attractive luster and drape.

Silk taffeta	A plain, closely woven, smooth fabric with a slight luster. Silk taffeta creates a beautiful effect when gathered for volume because of its light and airy qualities.
Vogue, April 1926	"For the young and lovely bride who adores the picturesque type of thing and can live up to it, taffeta suggests itself, crisp and bouffant over a skirt of silver lace and net."
Slipper satin	A fine satin with a dull surface finish that is often used for bridesmaids' ballet pumps.
Tulle	A very fine silk, cotton, or synthetic net or gauze. Tulle was originally used for petticoats and underskirts, but it is ideal for creating full-skirted ballerina gowns because of its frothy qualities that connote youthfulness and femininity.

FAIRY TALE

Brides Magazine, Summer 1960	"After years of make believe, your favorite fantasies grow up and become true."
Harper's Bazaar, February 1965	"Brides are blossoming younger, lovelier, more joyous than ever before. Dress to catch the wedding fun, prettier and more festive than Cinderella's ever was: whitest organdie with guipure lace."
John Galliano (b.1960), British fashion designer	"I want fashion to be beautiful, escapist, aspirational. Fairy godmothers are hard to come by so let me tell you: you shall go to the ball! Make life more of a fantasy and more of the story you imagined."
Paris Hilton (b.1981), American heiress and socialite	"I'd imagine my wedding as a fairy tale . . . huge, beautiful and white."

FASCINATOR

A decorative headpiece that usually comprises a comb, hair clip, or headband adorned with embellishments such as feathers, flowers, and jewels. Fascinators typically include a piece of netting that can partially veil the face.

Philip Treacy (b.1967), Irish milliner

"They're okay—I don't have a huge issue with them. But they're the lazy option. You don't have to be lazy! Ultimately, though, you have to just go with whatever makes you feel good."

FASHIONABLE

Harper's Bazaar, April 1903

"[Wedding gowns should be] toned down by good common sense. There are few women to whom these picturesque styles are becoming. . . . It is not possible merely to say this or that gown will be the thing to wear merely because it is fashionable; it must be becoming."

Suzy Menkes (b.1943), British fashion journalist (on Princess Diana's wedding dress, 1981)

"The delicacy of detail and of colour were the most surprising notes in an occasion when fashion is fairly predictable."

Vera Wang (b.1949), American bridal wear designer

"A love of style always precedes fashion."

FATHER OF THE BRIDE

The father of the bride plays an important role in a traditional wedding ceremony. While there is no longer an expectation for him to pay for the wedding and the reception, with many modern couples assuming the cost of the occasion themselves, the role of the father of the bride in "giving his daughter away" during the ceremony and dancing with her at the reception endures. The father of the bride may also speak at the reception. If the bride's father has passed away or is no longer a presence in her life, she may ask another male relative, close male friend, or her mother to assume this role.

Esquire Fashion Guide for All Occasions, 1957

"Escorts daughter in the processional. 'Gives bride away' at the ceremony. Dances with daughter after groom. Acts as host at the reception. Assumes financial responsibility for wedding, reception, transportation."

FAVORS

Token gifts given to guests at the wedding breakfast as a memento. Often these take the form of confectionary presented in a decorative bag or box. It was customary in Renaissance Italy to give guests sugar-coated almonds, and these remain a popular choice for those wishing to maintain the tradition. Often knotted ribbons are incorporated with wedding favors. Aside from their decorative qualities, knotted ribbons are symbolic of the enduring "knot" of love being tied between the bride and groom.

FLOWER GIRL

Vogue, May 1918

"The little flower girl counts the wedding one of the happiest events in a happy child['s] world."

The tradition of the bride being attended by a young flower girl dates back to ancient times. In Greek, Roman, and medieval culture, brides were accompanied by a girl who carried a sheaf of grain to symbolize the family's and community's hope for fertility. The Elizabethan association of children with hope and innocence also led to their being incorporated into the wedding party.

FLOWERS

The Cult of Fashion, 1902

"Next to the importance of wearing jewels and lace comes the wearing of flowers."

Mary Brooks Picken (1886–1981), American fashion writer

"Flowers, 'exquisite creatures' that they are, are beautiful always; but there are some cases where certain flowers, especially when worn by individuals, are more beautiful than others, and a certain combination of flowers is more pleasing and expresses individuality more than another."

Valentino (b.1932), Italian fashion designer

"Flowers for me are a great source of inspiration: I like to reproduce them on a dress, turning a woman into a bouquet.'"

Vogue, April 1926

"Cala-lilies are the appropriate flower—regal and formal and [as] clear cut as the bride's beauty."

Flower	Meaning
Apple blossom	Good fortune
Aster	Daintiness and love
Bluebells	Everlasting love
Camellia	"My destiny is in your hands"
Carnation (red)	Admiration
Carnation (white)	Ardent love
Chrysanthemum (red)	"I love you"
Chrysanthemum (white)	Truth
Delphinium	Luck
Forget-me-not	True love and remembrance
Honeysuckle	Generosity and affection
Ivy	Eternal fidelity
Lilac	Youthful innocence
Lily	Majesty
Lily-of-the-valley	Return of happiness
Myrtle	Love and remembrance
Orange blossom	Innocence and purity
Orchid	Fertility
Peony	Shyness
Phlox	Sweet dreams
Rose (coral)	Desire
Rose (dark pink)	Gratitude
Rose (light pink)	Grace
Rose (red)	Love and passion
Rose (white)	Innocence
Rose (yellow)	Friendship
Sweet pea	Delicate pleasures
Violets	Faithfulness
White carnations	Honesty

is for GROOM

GALLIANO, JOHN

John Galliano (b.1960) is an award-winning British fashion designer known for intensely romantic couture and ready-to-wear evening gowns. Galliano combines technical precision with a deep interest in historical dress to create designs that focus on the handcraft of haute couture. In addition to his own label, Galliano fulfilled the role of chief designer at Givenchy (July 1995–October 1996) and Christian Dior (October 1996–March 2011). In 2002 he created a two-tone, dip-dyed pink-and-white dress for No Doubt singer Gwen Stefani's wedding to Gavin Rossdale.

GARTER

Garters were popular during the seventeenth and eighteenth centuries and comprised delicate silk sashes tied just below the knee. It was customary for a bride to undo her garters as she entered the bridal chamber and to let them hang down as a symbol of her intent to consummate the marriage. Traditionally garters are blue, the color associated with the Virgin Mary. Many modern brides continue the custom of wearing a garter, although it now takes the form of an elasticized satin, lace, or net band that sits on the thigh. Blue is often still incorporated into the design, making garters a popular choice for fulfilling the "something blue" element of the bride's attire.

GIFT REGISTRY

Giving gifts at a wedding is a long-established custom around the world. Traditionally, these included food and household items to help the new couple set up a home. Now, when many couples already live together before they marry, money, especially a contribution to the honeymoon, is an increasingly popular choice in lieu of a gift. Handmade gifts are still treasured for their personal qualities. Among the gifts that the Queen of England treasured the most when she married Prince Philip in 1947 was a fine shawl knitted for her by Mahatma Gandhi.

GIFTS

It is customary for the bride to present her bridesmaids with a token of thanks and appreciation, and for the groom to do the same for his best man and ushers. Sometimes these gifts are given at a rehearsal dinner, especially if they take the form of jewelry or another accessory that should be worn for the wedding. It is also popular to present these gifts during the speeches at the wedding breakfast.

Marianne Ostier (1902–76), American jewelry designer

"Among appropriate gifts are gold charm bracelets, cigarette boxes, powder compacts, lipstick holders and the like. These should be engraved with the date of the wedding, the name of the happy couple and a memorable phrase. If the jewels are too small to be engraved, the box should be embossed in a similar manner.

The groom, in a similar fashion and with the same engraving, makes his gifts to the best man and ushers. In gold he may choose tiepins and clips, cuff links, money clips, key chains, toothpicks. Pencil[s] or fountain pens are appropriate, or silver letter openers, with the box or the article bearing the signs of the occasion."

The bride and groom also often exchange gifts on the occasion of their wedding—jewelry and watches are popular choices.

Esquire Fashion Guide for All Occasions, 1957

"Be certain that when you buy a present for your bride, it is something for her adornment; nothing else is proper. It should be of an enduring quality in remembrance of this event."

GIMMAL

A particular type of wedding ring popular in the Elizabethan era for its romantic resonance; gimmals comprised three interlocking bands. One band was worn by the bride, the second by the groom, and the third by a close friend who acted as witness to the marriage. At the wedding ceremony the three bands were reunited and placed on the bride's finger.

GROOM

The success of hit television series *Mad Men* has sparked an interest in 1960s fashions. The *Esquire Fashion Guide for All Occasions* has some useful pointers for grooms who wish to greet their bride in the sartorial style of the show's debonair star Don Draper (see overleaf).

Wedding Etiquette, 1966

"In past generations and even today in fashionable weddings, the bridegroom will wear a black tail coat, a black waistcoat, a pair of pin-striped trousers, a silk hat, light spats, a tie with a quiet pattern on a black ground, and he should carry a pair of grey suede gloves."

Esquire Fashion Guide for All Occasions, 1957

"If the wedding is a formal day[time] affair, it is customary that you provide ascot ties, stock pins, waistcoats, and gloves for your wedding party; this is to ensure uniformity of appearance. . . . Your tie and the one for the best man should be of identical design."

Hair	Suits	Shirts	Ties	Hats
Fair	Blue-grays are best, blue-greens and reddish browns following. With pale skin, avoid tans and gray-greens. Dark blues are good with fair or ruddy complexions.	Choose colors that are lighter than the suits. Carry some of the blue or gray into your shirts.	Subdued colors are best with small figures or larger individual patterns.	Grays are good, medium browns, too. Be careful of dark browns and drab greens.
Black	If you don't have a dark gray suit, get one fast. Browns in medium shades are okay if complexion is ruddy or tanned.	Shades of cream or tan are fine for dark complexions but not for pale faces.	Bright ties in patterns and stripes should be complementary to you.	Medium shades of tan or gray will suit you best. Avoid dark tones of brown or any very dark shades.
Gray	Dark blue is your best color. Blue-gray is good with pale skin, Oxford gray for the ruddy type. Most browns are unbecoming.	Pale tones look best. Blues are excellent. Take it easy with tans.	Conservative colors are generally best, but try matching some vivid shades against your own coloring.	Brown is bad unless it's a red or rust brown. Stay with grays or medium greens.
Red	Warm browns, blues, and dark grays in that order are all very good. Be careful with very light grays.	Blue and green tints are always good. Stick to pale shades in yellow.	Green is perfect. Go light on reds, yellows, and orange shades. Almost any other color is OK.	Browns and dark greens will be complementary. Medium or dark shades of gray come second.
Brown	Mid-tones of gray, tan, and brown are your colors. Blues are also good. Avoid very dark browns.	You look your best in a blue shirt, but experiment with other pale shades.	Let your complexion be your guide. If it's ruddy, soft colors are best. Go easy on greens if you are pale-skinned.	Browns, greens, or grays in medium tones are for you. Don't match the brown in your hair too closely.

Suit	Shirt	Ties	Socks	Shoes	Hats	Handkerchiefs	Belts
Blue	Maroon and white	Blue and gold	Dark red	Black	Gray	Maroon and white	Blue
	Gray	Red and gray	Blue	Dark brown	Blue-gray	Red and gray	Dark gray
	Blue, gray, and white	Red and yellow	Blue	Dark brown	Brown	Blue and gray	Black
	Yellow	Blue and dark red	Dark gray	Black	Blue	Blue and white	Black
Gray	Green	Red and green	Green	Dark brown	Grayish green	Green and white	Gray
	Blue and white	Red and blue	Blue	Dark brown	Blue	Blue and white	Blue
	Red, gray, and white	Blue and gray	White	Black	Gray	Red, gray, and white	Brown
	Coral	Black	Black	Black	Black	White	Black
Brown	Tan	Red and gold	Maroon	Dark brown	Green	Red and white	Brown
	Green and white	Copper	Green	Dark brown	Brown	Green and white	Brown
	Brown and white	Green and yellow	Brown	Dark brown	Brown	Brown and white	Olive
	Ivory	Red and green	Maroon	Dark brown	Olive	Red, yellow, and white	Olive
Green	Tan	Brown and gold	Brown	Brown	Brown	Tan and white	Brown
	Red and white	Green	Maroon	Brown	Olive	Maroon and white	Brown
	Green and white	Copper	Green	Brown	Green	Brown and white	Olive
	Gray	Red and gray	Gray	Black	Gray	Red, gray, and white	Olive

| Marianne Ostier (1902–76), American jewelry designer | "Every business or professional man is aware of the importance of a proper appearance. Many, however, do not have the time a woman has to shop and weigh and consider. . . . It is thus often the wife's role to see that her husband is properly equipped." |

GROOMING

Every bride wants to look her best on her wedding day. No matter how casual the approach, most brides will undergo some form of beauty treatment or preparation to ensure they walk down the aisle looking and feeling stunning.

| *Harper's Bazaar*, May 1952 | "Grooming must be impeccable and started in time. Not a hair of your eyebrow out of place; not a hair in the wrong place on your legs." |

| *Vogue*, April 1940 | "Be your own dream of yourself—as calm and lovely and fragrant as a Graustarkian princess. If you're to be married at four, don't get up until eleven. If you wake up early, you well may brush your teeth and drink your lemon-and-water if you like, but tumble back into bed. The bolster of a few hours' additional rest will keep any strain lines out of your face." |

| *Harper's Bazaar*, February 1960 | "[The] 1960s bride aspires to something more than grooming, more even than prettiness; no less than the look of perfection. Achieving this look takes time above all things: minimum—one month." |

"All will be well so long as he does not see his bride in bridal attire before he meets her at the altar, does not let his hat fall, does not drop the ring or put it only partially on his bride's finger. If she has to assist him in this matter then he may expect to be ruled by her in the future."

Wedding Etiquette, 1966

is for HISTORICAL

"I really loved the '20s and the whole
Art Deco time. . . . I just think it was the
most amazing time for style and design."
Jenny Packham (b.1965), British fashion designer

HAIR

It was fashionable from the fourteenth to the seventeenth centuries for brides to wear their hair loose, as a symbol of their virginity.

Like wedding gowns, there is a virtually unending list of options when it comes to bridal hairstyles. Some brides like to indulge in a special updo to offset the glamour and dramatic effect of their gown; others prefer something more natural and less sculpted. A bridal hairstyle must, however, take into consideration any headdress that is to be worn, whether this is a tiara, ornamental hairpin, or an arrangement of fresh flowers. The style of veil selected, if there is to be one, will also have a bearing on the way the hair can be styled.

Jenny Packham (b.1965), British fashion designer

"I always think of the groom turning around and seeing someone with curly hair who's always got straight hair, you know? Must be a bit of a shock."

HATINATOR

A hybrid of the hat and the fascinator; also referred to as the "cocktail hat." Hatinators usually consist of a structured base on a headband, rather than a full crown and hatband. Hatinators often sit well away from the face, which makes them easier to wear and more flattering than a full hat, allowing more of the face to be seen.

HEADDRESS

Headdresses comprise ornaments that are worn in the hair. They are sometimes worn alone, but often they are used to hold a veil in place. In the Victorian period it was popular for brides to attach their veils to a bonnet, while the 1920s bride often attached her veil to a cloche hat. It was also popular for brides in the 1920s to have clusters of flowers worn over

each ear that were attached to long, floating veils of
tulle. Tiaras, crowns, headbands, and wreaths have
also endured as popular selections. In the 1960s the
fashion for a headdress of orange blossom gave way
to a vogue for wearing a spray of crisp tulle fixed to
the top of the head with a single large flower.

Brides Magazine, Summer 1962

"Your headdress . . . must be hand-in-glove with
your wedding dress. Just as important is that it
should be perfect for you, work along with your face
and hairstyle toward one beautiful look."

The Times, March 29, 1920

"A wreath may be worn in the hair, but it is more
fashionable to wear jewels in the hair and a flower
belt around the waist, in which case the flowers
are artificial."

HEIGHT

Genevieve Antoine
Dariaux (b.1914), French
author on etiquette

"Tall, thin brides will find it advantageous to
accentuate their sculptural beauty by dressing in a
sheath of heavy material with a *manteau de cour*—a
sort of cape attached to the shoulders—which forms
a train; long sleeves; and a simple diadem in their
hair. Small, very young brides would do better to
place the accent on their doll-like charm by wearing
a wedding dress of tulle, lace, or organdy in the
summer, with a full, puffed skirt, no train, little
short sleeves, short white gloves, and a headdress
or bonnet that adds to their height."

Vogue, April 1926

"For the tall and striking bride who is truly
sophisticated, one sees white satin, severely simple,
long-sleeved, with a train of satin and a Russian
headdress."

Vogue, February 1930

"*Vogue* suggests that the bride study very carefully the effect of her veil in relation to her height before she determines its length, as a very long veil on a very short bride, or a very short veil on a very tall bride, gives an unbalanced and asymmetrical effect that is most unfortunate at this time."

HISTORICAL STYLES

Victorian (1837–1901)

Voluminous skirts adorned with flounces of satin and lace are classically associated with the Victorian wedding dress. The full-skirted look was achieved with layers of petticoats or, from 1856, the crinoline (see page 27), which supported the fashionable silhouette without the need for layers of underskirts. Bodices were fitted and tapered to a narrow waist, and sleeves were often longer with wide cuffs and fringes or trimmings of lace. A white wedding dress, veil, and wreath of orange blossoms became established staples of bridal attire in the period.

Edwardian (1901–10)

Edwardian wedding dresses were characterized by paneled skirts shaped over the hips and flared to the ankles. Attention was focused on the back of the dress, with wider panels forming a train. Edwardian wedding gowns often featured a high neckline, which was a popular feature of day-wear designs, although for the wedding dress it was often constructed from a sheer fabric or lace.

1910s

Informal, lean lines and elaborate detailing and ornamentation characterized the silhouette and style of wedding dresses of the late 1910s. Delicate overdresses and ethereal draperies created from lace, embroidery, and pearls were the height of fashion for bridal attire. In 1917 *Vogue* lamented, "Will it never return . . . that chaste garment, severely plain with its stark, gleaming train?"

1920s

An innovation of the period credited to the French couturier Coco Chanel (1883–1971) was the short wedding dress, which hung to just below the knee and was worn with a long train attached to the shoulders.

The prevailing silhouette of the 1920s, however, was a loose-fitting, sleeveless chemise dress with low, dropped waist and a high, scooped neck. The shape and surface embellishment frequently referenced the Art Deco artistic movement with bold, geometric shapes and lavish ornamentation, often in heavy embroidery and beads.

The narrow silhouette of the chemise dress required less fabric than full-skirted gowns, meaning expensive cloth could be used economically. Chemise dresses required fluid fabrics that would drape well, such as georgette, silk-satin, and crêpe de Chine. Another popular choice was Jeanne Lanvin's (1867–1946) *robe de style* (pictured left), which was characterized by its full skirt and long, loose sleeves.

The Times, March 29, 1920

"The conventional wedding dress of white satin and orange blossoms is being gradually replaced by something less conservative and uniform."

Vogue, April 1921

"A gown for a very modern bride has no sleeves and very little back, for its pointed décolleté comes to the low waist-line."

Vogue, April 1922
(on the wedding gown
Paul Poiret designed for
his niece's wedding)

"Out of the shimmer of brocade and the sparkle of silver cloth, Paul Poiret has created for the April bride a wedding gown which has caught the iridescence of waves breaking into spray in sunlight. The sleeves display a delightful originality in being shirred to a deep shoulder-line and East meets West when the Occidental bride winds the long tulle veil into a turban about her head."

1930s

Hollywood glamour influenced wedding dresses in the 1930s, with many brides choosing the soft, draping crêpes and shiny satins that clung to the curves of their favorite screen stars. As with most evening dresses of the period, bridal gowns tended to be cut on the bias to flatter the natural lines of the body. The epic and historical films of the decade also influenced bridal wear, as medieval details, such as long sleeves with wide, open cuffs, were incorporated into some designs. Cowl necklines were another popular feature that added a soft, romantic touch.

Vogue, 1930

"The bride appears at her loveliest in the new fitted and moulded gowns with long, sweeping lines."

"The look was still very neat-headed, with long swathes of tulle or fine lace silhouetting an intricately cut yet simple dress."

1940s

Many brides who desired a traditional wedding gown opted for creations made out of parachute silk, which was not subject to rationing restrictions. The fashionable silhouette incorporated a broad shoulder-line and a full-length gown. Owing to material shortages, skirts were not full, but they often included several gathers and so were not overly narrow, either. Gowns tended to include long sleeves as well as an element of decorative detailing between the waist and bust, which created an illusion of gentle curves.

For practical reasons, many wartime brides chose instead a smart, tailored, two-piece suit, consisting of a fitted jacket and a narrow skirt to just below the knee. These were either from their wardrobe or a sensible purchase with their coupon allowance that could be worn again.

1950s

As wartime clothing restrictions were lifted, wedding dresses could once again utilize more cloth. This was demonstrated in bridal styles with full skirts and fitted bodices that echoed Christian Dior's (1905–1957) fashionable "New Look." Another popular wedding silhouette of the 1950s presented a mid-calf dress that emphasized the natural waistline and bust. Special underwear was vital in achieving these silhouettes, including a crinoline, or net petticoat, and a strapless waist-cincher that pulled the body into an hourglass figure and smoothed the line over the hip.

"Fragile delicacy and a deliciously gentle femininity epitomized the sought-after bridal look of the 1950s."

"Nylon was the wedding discovery of the decade. Far less expensive than silk and with the 'white-white' that could only be attained in synthetic fabrics."

1960s

Synthetic fabrics such as nylon and rayon had lost their novelty by the early 1960s, and there was a reversion to simple lines and classic styles in plain and heavy slubbed silks and satins. While many brides opted for a traditional, full-length gown, British fashion designer Mary Quant's (b.1934) minidresses also made an impact on bridal attire.

More generally, the youthful and experimental nature of 1960s street fashions carried through into bridal wear. While French fashion designer Yves Saint Laurent (1936–2008) designed a skimpy, flower-studded bikini for the daring bride-to-be, other alternatives to the classic wedding dress included paper minidresses and transparent gowns intended to be worn over minimal undergarments.

Vogue, 1961

"This year's weddings are distinguished by new clear-cut simplicity ... unclustered outlines (no frills), stiff veils (short enough to spring up with bouffancy above a sleek hairstyle), [and] crisp materials (rippling fabrics don't take firm shapes in the same way)."

Vogue, 1964

"Wedding dresses have less and less fuss to distract attention from the bride's face: they are gentler, dreamier and simpler than before."

HONEYMOON

The term "honeymoon" derives from the custom practiced in Scandinavia of giving newlyweds mead, an alcoholic drink made from fermented honey. This was to be consumed every day for the first month, or "moon," of marriage.

The honeymoon served a practical purpose for many couples married when incidences of arranged marriages were high. For newlyweds in this category, the honeymoon afforded a much-needed opportunity to get to know one another. Only with the increase in companionate marriages was the honeymoon accorded romantic connotations— and only in the nineteenth century, when technologies advanced in rail and steam travel, did the honeymoon become firmly associated with a trip away.

is for INVITATIONS

IMPRACTICAL

Many brides-to-be aspire to cause a sensation and, in doing so, select something "different" or are tempted by gowns and accessories that are not entirely practical for a day-long celebration.

The actress Jayne Mansfield wowed her guests in a stunning, mermaid-style lace gown that showed off her voluptuous curves when she married Mickey Hargitay in 1958; but the skintight dress was so restrictive, she could barely walk. *Real Housewives of Atlanta* star Kim Zolciak also struggled to move at her 2011 wedding in her Baracci dress, which was covered in Swarovski crystals, pearls, and beads and weighed 32 pounds (14.5 kg).

In 2007 Chinese bride Xie Qiyun won a competition that no one else would want to enter when she got married with a train that measured 650 feet (200.8 m) and weighed 220 pounds (100 kg).

INDIVIDUAL

Every bride will be unique—because she brings to her wedding her own sense of style and identity.

Vogue, 1923

"Fashion has supplanted custom and individuality has supplanted both."

Vera Wang (b.1949),
American bridal wear designer

"A wedding gown should fulfill the bride's own sense of identity."

INVITATIONS

Many modern invitations eschew traditional wedding stationery, with its embossed monograms and calligraphic script, in favor of a bespoke approach. This can range from filling envelopes with flower petals or incorporating romantic excerpts from sheet music, to commissioning an artist to create a personalized glass etching of the wedding venue to stamp with. Some people prefer a simple approach and opt for an invitation printed from a home computer. Whereas it used to be customary for the invitation to a wedding to come from the bride's parents, many couples now extend their own invitation to their prospective guests.

Vogue, April 1935 — "Wedding invitations must be primarily of the best quality. They can be of medium size that folds once, such as Number engraved on Strathmore's 'Carillon,' which is particularly smart at the moment. The sheet slips into the envelope without folding and is engraved on Linweave's 'Haviland,' which has the rich glaze of Haviland china and a great deal of dignity."

Vogue's Book of Etiquette and Good Manners, 1969 — "A formal invitation may be written by hand, fully engraved, or partially engraved, and it is always worded in the third person."

Wedding Etiquette, 1966 — "The invitations to a wedding should be issued well in advance of the ceremony—at least two weeks before, three being quite usual. . . . The invitation is always written in the third person, never in the first. It should be printed for preference, and a copperplate will be used for the purpose."

J *is for* JULIET CAP

JEWELRY

Decorative objects worn as accessories either on garments (brooches and pins) or about the body (necklaces, rings, bracelets, and earrings). Today there is a huge market in costume jewelry that uses manufactured gemstones and synthetic materials and pastes to create the sparkle and appearance of authentic precious stones.

Marianne Ostier (1902–76), American jewelry designer

"The bride, and especially at the formal evening wedding, will wear jewelry only in white: diamonds or pearls. Jewels should be modest and few."

"If a bracelet is worn, it should be on the right arm. The left arm and hand should be bare of ornament, the engagement ring being transferred, before the service, to stay on the right hand, before the groom has slipped the wedding band on his bride's finger."

"No wristwatch should be worn; on this night the groom is guardian of the hours."

JULIET CAP

A small skullcap that fits closely over the veil. The cap usually consists of a wide, open mesh, although it is sometimes made of the same fabric as the wedding gown and might be embellished with pearls or other jewels, beading, or embroidery. The headpiece became so called because of its similarity to the caps worn onstage by Shakespeare's Juliet.

Vogue, December 1906

"The Juliet cap is entrancing and calls for a low, girlish arrangement of the hair, twisted and knotted on the neck."

is for KILLER HEELS

KELLY, GRACE

Grace Kelly's wedding in 1956 to Prince Rainier III of Monaco caused a worldwide sensation. A television audience of more than thirty million watched the American actress become Princess Grace in an outfit that incorporated more than a mile of *peau de soie* (luxury grosgrain silk) and lace. The ensemble consisted of a dress with lace bodice, under-bodice, and a skirt supported by two petticoats, as well as a headdress, elbow-length veil trimmed with lace, and a lace-and-pearl–encrusted prayer book. The dress, conceived by Helen Rose (1904–85), an American costume designer, has endured as an inspiration. Similarities were drawn between Princess Grace's gown and that worn by Kate Middleton for her wedding to Prince William in April 2011.

KILLER HEELS

Shoes, often stilettos, with heels of 4 inches (10 cm) or more. Killer heels are so called because they give the appearance of longer legs and a sleeker, sexier silhouette—but also because they are characteristically uncomfortable to wear. Brides wearing shorter dresses who wish to add height and make their legs appear slender may consider them, but a shorter heel offers a much more sensible option for those who value comfort and a more modest style.

KILT

An article of traditional Scottish male attire that takes the form of a skirt of pleated tartan fabric wrapped around the body and held in place near the hem with a kilt pin. Many Scottish grooms, groomsmen, and even male wedding guests choose to wear kilts on the occasion of a wedding. It is customary for the tartan to be of the pattern associated with the wearer's family name or clan.

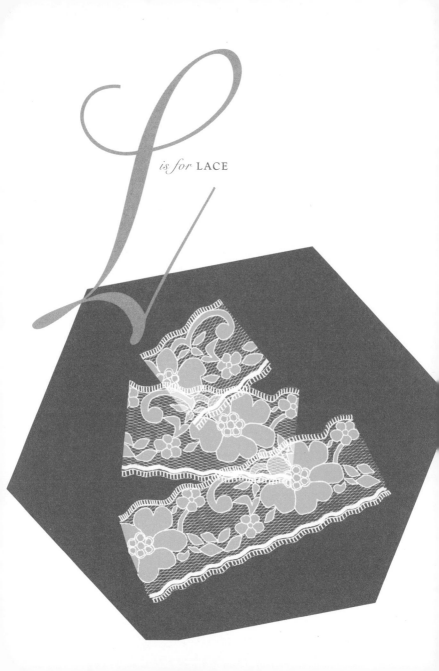

L *is for* LACE

LACE

Vogue, February 1930

"Lace is surely the queen of fabrics, and although it has suffered, in this democratic age, the partial eclipse of other royalties, it is nowhere more appropriate than on the bride."

Lace has long been considered a staple of bridal and special-occasion wear because of its inherent delicacy. The skill and time involved in handcrafting lace also made it scarce and, thus, costly and special. Until recent decades, it was popular for trimmings of bridal lace to be passed down through the generations for future brides in the family.

Lace is an openwork fabric with patterns created by holes formed by machine or hand. There are many types of lace that possess different textural and decorative qualities. Traditionally linen, silk, and gold and silver threads were used in the production of lace, although cotton is a popular modern choice. A few examples of different types of lace are: Brussels lace (a bobbin lace wherein the pattern is worked prior to the ground being added); Alençon lace (a needle lace that emerged in the sixteenth century and quickly became known as the "queen of lace"); Chantilly lace (a delicate and fragile handmade bobbin lace); and *mezza mandolina* (a delicate lace with a fine, cobwebby appearance). Honiton lace, produced in the Devonshire village of that name, was selected by Queen Victoria for the trimmings of her wedding gown; since then, Honiton lace has become synonymous with bridal attire.

Synthetic lace has made the fabric a more affordable option. Although contemporary manufacturing techniques are capable of producing refined and delicate designs of high quality, cheap versions can be very noticeable. Certainly nothing can match the cachet of handmade lace, and the allure of a gown incorporating vintage lace endures among many modern brides-to-be.

Madeleine Ginsburg (b.1928), British fashion curator

"Lace, always an expensive accessory and often a gift from the bride's family, seems to acquire the tradition of an heirloom and tends to come to us detached from the wedding outfit that it once accompanied."

Edwina Ehrman (b.1953), British fashion curator

"Lace's delicate, airy patterns veiled and enhanced the skin and provided a counterpoint to rich and lustrous dress silks."

LACROIX, CHRISTIAN

Christian Lacroix (b.1951) is a French fashion designer renowned for his haute couture bridal wear collections. Most French houses typically design only three or four wedding dresses a year, with the bulk of commissions coming from clients in the Middle and Far East or from titled Europeans. However, bridal wear accounts for 40 percent of Lacroix commissions—the house received orders for eighteen couture bridal gowns in 1992 and twelve in 1993. In 1994 the cost of a Lacroix couture bridal gown ranged between $25,000 and $100,000. His style incorporates bold silhouettes overlaid with color, texture, and elaborate ornamentation. Lacroix attracts a clientele of a host of celebrities and Hollywood stars.

LANVIN, JEANNE-MARIE

Jeanne-Marie Lanvin (1867–1946) was a French fashion designer who founded the House of Lanvin. She is considered one of the most influential designers of the 1920s and 1930s.

Vogue, May 1916 "Mme Lanvin created a most charming wedding gown (but then, Lanvin creations are always charming) for a recent bride. The simple satin frock possesses all the surprising little touches for which Lanvin frocks are so remarkable. The basque with its quaint seams, the simplicity of the trimming— satin loops applied in delicate rows with delicate sprays of orange blossom—and even the reinforced hem all reveal Lanvin in every line. There is something distinctly new in this silhouette. We have had the distended skirt before (it is Lanvin's own), but in the basque and the tight sleeve there is something interestingly new."

LINGERIE

From the French *linges*, meaning "washables," "lingerie" refers to women's high-quality underwear, frequently of a particularly alluring nature. Often the garments are made from sensuous materials such as satin and lace.

Vogue, April 1919 "One of the most understandable of feminine foibles is lingerie of lacy sheerness and frail pale colors."

The Complete Guide to Wedding Etiquette, 1960 "The most important part is the 'bridal set,' comprising: negligee, nightgown, slip, and panties. The bride should also have a second-best set, and a tailored set, for everyday wear. Other useful articles are: housecoat, bedroom slippers, slips, stockings, panties, bed jacket, girdles, brassieres and pyjamas."

Vogue, April 1919 "Alluring laces and ribbons combine to tempt the indulged young bride."

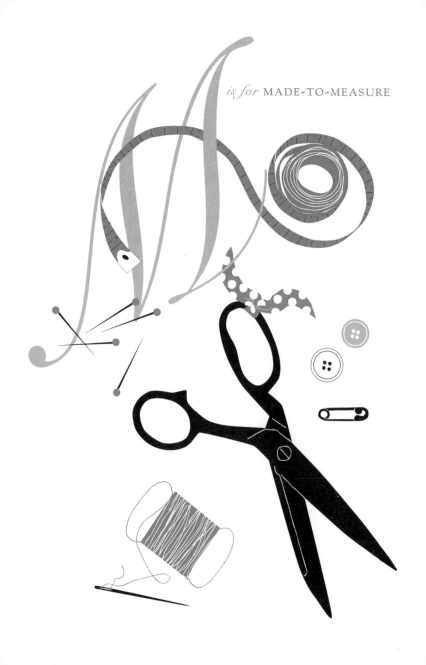

is for MADE-TO-MEASURE

MADE-TO-MEASURE

Custom-made gowns created for an individual client to her specific measurements by a designer or fashion house. These can range from the humblest local dressmaker to an internationally renowned designer. Most established designers are recognized for having their own particular bridal style.

MAID OF HONOR

The principal bridesmaid, usually the bride's closest friend or older sister. Traditionally, the maid of honor helped the bride dress for her wedding and, later, her honeymoon. She also acted as one of the legal witnesses at the wedding ceremony and undertook pre-wedding tasks such as organizing a bridal shower or bachelorette party. Most modern brides tend not to make distinctions between their adult bridesmaids, although for practical reasons the bride's closest friend may still take on the task of organizing the bachelorette party.

MAIDEN NAME

The surname of the bride before marriage, if she assumes her husband's name after the ceremony.

The tradition for women to adopt their husband's surname dates back to when a bride passed from the control of her father to that of her husband upon marriage. In the eighteenth century it sometimes occurred that the husband would adopt his wife's name if her family was of higher social standing.

Although the tradition endures, many questions concerning identity, self-preservation, and gender equality are now part of the bride's decision. Linking surnames with a hyphen to "double-barrel" them is a compromise growing in popularity.

MAIL ORDER

Mail-order wedding dresses were a popular choice in the 1960s for brides seeking to reconcile their dreams with their budget. These dresses were an affordable alternative to bespoke gowns and outfits from specialty boutiques, as they circumvented the price markups that were added by the stores.

Advertisement for Lipmans mail-order wedding dresses, in *Brides Magazine*, Summer 1962

"Only Lipmans of Nottingham offer the Magic Key to a Dream Wedding. For now these famous Lipmans gowns can be ordered by post! Compare these prices—made possible only because they come to you direct from Nottingham."

MAKEUP

Vogue, July 1956

"Realize that from the time you go down the aisle on your father's arm, until the time you dress in your going-away clothes after the reception, there may not be a moment for retouching makeup."

Cosmetics, including foundation, blusher, lipstick, and eye shadow, that are applied to the face to define and enhance natural features. Some women are comfortable wearing heavy makeup on a daily basis, while for others their wedding day may be one of a few occasions in their life when they wear any at all. The prevailing current opinion is that less is more where bridal makeup is concerned, with a natural look usually being the preferred style.

Harper's Bazaar, May 1952

"Makeup for the bride should be pink and white and delicate as apple blossom."

Harper's Bazaar, May 1952

"Touch your cheeks with the merest bloom of rouge, and rely for the rest on powder artfully laid over a lasting foundation."

Vogue, April 1940 "Even if you are a dark lipstick addict, don't wear it against a background of lace and tulle. Your mouth will look hard and sore."

MATURE BRIDES

Vogue, April 1921 "The difficult problem of how the mature bride may achieve distinction is solved by a gown of silver lace and dark velvet. . . ."

Vera Wang (b.1949), American bridal wear designer "When I decided to get married at forty, I couldn't find a dress with the modernity or sophistication I wanted. That's when I saw the opportunity for a wedding gown business."

MIDDLETON, KATE (CATHERINE, DUCHESS OF CAMBRIDGE)

Kate Middleton's choice of couturier for her wedding gown, British designer Sarah Burton (b.1974), Creative Director at Alexander McQueen, was declared a triumph. The dress was constructed from ivory and white satin gazar (a loosely woven silk with a crisp finish) and was hand-stitched at the Royal School of Needlework. Middleton's choice of British designers and craftsmen echoed that of Queen Victoria almost 175 years before. The design was inspired by the *peau de soie* and lace gown Grace Kelly wore in 1956 for her marriage to Prince Rainier III of Monaco. Middleton's skirt, which evoked the petals of a flower in bloom, also bore a subtle resemblance to the work of Anglo-American fashion designer Charles James (1906–78), who was renowned for designs that explored natural, particularly botanical, forms.

Sarah Burton (b.1974), British fashion designer and Creative Director at Alexander McQueen "It has been the experience of a lifetime to work with Catherine Middleton to create her wedding dress, and I have enjoyed every moment of it."

MISTAKE

Vogue, April 1925 "The reason why so many brides wear the wrong thing is, undoubtedly, because they haven't had the necessary practice."

MORNING SUIT

The daytime formal dress code for men—an ensemble consisting of a morning coat, waistcoat, and striped trousers—often worn by the groom and male members of the wedding party. Men may also wear a variant wherein all components are the same color and material, often gray; this is only considered properly appropriate on the occasion of a wedding or at the races.

MOSS BROS

Wedding-dress rental services became established soon after World War II as an option for brides facing fabric shortages and subsequently expensive materials. Moss Bros, which had been renting out men's formal clothes and uniforms since the 1890s, was the first British company to offer a bridal wear rental service. The company began purchasing dresses in the years of postwar austerity with its coupon reserve, enabling brides to rent a dress for around half the price of purchasing one. The company also offered a selection of outfits for bridesmaids and pages. In the 1950s and 1960s the most popular rental dresses were expensive couture creations from Paris. Although Moss Bros now deals exclusively with menswear, the chain remains a popular option for grooms and groomsmen wishing to rent formal wear.

Advertisement for Bride-Be-Lovely bridal rental service in *Brides Magazine*, Spring 1962 "You can have a once-in-a-lifetime wedding dress, and no worry over what to do with it afterwards."

MOTHER-IN-LAW

The mother-in-law relationship has historically been associated with difficulty and tension. Satirized as interfering monsters who are impossible to please, mother-in-law characters often appear as the subject of many jokes concerning marriage.

Vera Wang (b.1949), American bridal wear designer

"Difficulty can also arise between a bride-to-be and her prospective mother-in-law. The relationship between the 'first lady' of a man's life and her successor may be fraught with tension."

Les Dawson (1931–93), British comedian

"My mother-in-law fell down a wishing well. I was amazed; I never knew they worked."

MOTHER OF THE BRIDE

Marianne Ostier (1902–76), American jewelry designer

"As every mother knows, her proudest moment is not that of her own wedding, but that when she watches her daughter being wed. That is the altar of her dreams."

Vogue, August 2001

"She's best supporting actress on the big day and needs to dress for the role."

Marianne Ostier (1902–76), American jewelry designer

"The bride is adorned for the occasion, the mother is adorned for her guests."

MYRTLE

The tradition of including a sprig of myrtle in royal wedding bouquets is a German custom that started with Queen Victoria's eldest daughter, Princess Victoria (the Princess Royal). When Victoria's sister Princess Alexandra married, a sprig was selected from the same bush. The bush—and its successors—have continued to supply royal bouquets until the present day.

N is for NAIL POLISH

NAIL POLISH

The custom of painting nails with a colored varnish dates back to Ancient Egypt and China, when women created polishes from natural substances. Modern nail polish appeared in the 1920s and was popularized by Hollywood. Many brides prefer to have polished yet uncolored nails for their wedding day, or a pale pink polish, or perhaps a "French" polish that highlights the white tips of the nail under a coat of pale pink.

Harper's Bazaar, May 1952

"Work on your hands weeks in advance. Select a clear or pale pink polish. This is not the moment for brilliant fingertips!"

Vogue, April 1940

"Use blush rose polish, too, for against the white of your sleeve, very dark polish somehow manages to make your hands look grimy."

Marianne Ostier (1902–76), American jewelry designer

"More than once, in selecting a ring, a woman has rejected one that was quite beautiful because it did not look well on her hands. This is an excellent reason—if the hands were not prejudiced by the nail polish. The polish should be fitted to the ring, not the ring to the polish."

NUPTIAL

From Old French, or from the Latin *nuptialis*, meaning "relating to marriage or a wedding." It is often used today when referring to a prenuptial contract, or "prenup," an agreement intended to protect the couple's independent assets should the marriage subsequently dissolve.

Gene Perret, screenwriter

"We have the greatest pre-nuptial agreement in the world. It's called love."

is for ORANGE BLOSSOM

ORANGE BLOSSOM

Orange blossom is a traditional element of the bridal ensemble. It was originally grown in the Holy Land, where it was considered a symbol of purity, innocence, and religious observance. Orange blossom is also associated with ancient Roman culture and is said to represent Juno's gift to Jupiter on their wedding day.

ORNAMENTATION

Articles added to an object to provide decoration; the action of decorating something or making it more elaborate.

Ornamentation as applied to fashion can take one of two forms: either items that are added to the surface of the fabric, such as piping, bows, flowers, buttons, and trimmings; or adornment engineered into the fabric, such as embroidery, beading, and painting.

OVER THE TOP

When Kanye West married American reality-television star Kim Kardashian in May 2014, the bride wore a Givenchy Haute Couture gown custom designed by Riccardo Tisci at an estimated cost of $500,000. Their daughter, North West, wore a matching handmade miniature version of the gown. The rare flowers used for their nuptials reportedly cost $136,000. Additionally, guests traveled from Paris to Florence to enjoy an array of activities surrounding the ceremony.

OVERWHELMING

Youth's Companion, 1904

"O Dick, it's no use! I can't marry you! It's, it's— oh, it's too much work!"

P *is for* PHOTOGRAPHER

PACKHAM, JENNY

Jenny Packham (b.1965) is an award-winning British fashion designer who specializes in evening and bridal wear. Her delicate, though often heavily embellished, gowns are a favorite among red-carpet stars, including Angelina Jolie, Eva Longoria, Kate Winslet, and Reese Witherspoon. The Duchess of Cambridge wears her designs regularly.

Jenny Packham (b.1965), British fashion designer

"If I look at dresses that I like from my designs and other collections, they usually have an attitude behind them, a subtle attitude that would make the woman wearing it feel very confident. Sometimes it is an amazing color; sometimes it's the beading or the cut."

PARACHUTE SILK

A popular choice of fabric for wartime wedding dresses, because it was not controlled under rationing restrictions. Parachute silk, which was made from the new synthetic fabric nylon, was originally used to manufacture military parachutes but was made available to consumers by 1945. The white fabric came in triangular sections and had to be cut on the bias, or across the weave of the fabric, which gave an elegant and flattering line to the dress. While these characteristics made it an instinctive choice for wartime wedding dresses, its slippery texture made it particularly difficult to handle and to sew.

PARIS

Vogue, May 1916

"Marriages may be made in heaven, but the wedding garments must come from Paris. . . . There is a certain magic in the mark 'Paris' that gives to filmy things an added grace, a more subtle charm, a mysterious something . . . a something which creates enduring envy in the hearts of those who have not and fills the hearts of those who have with great content."

PHOTOGRAPHER

Securing the services of a reputable photographer to record and capture the wedding ceremony and celebrations is a primary consideration for many couples. A photographer experienced in wedding photography will account for a sizeable amount of any wedding budget, especially as he or she will often spend most of the day recording events—from the bride getting dressed to the final farewells. Couples should consider in advance the particular shots and style they desire (posed portraits, spontaneous, or a mixture of both), and whether they would like photographs in black-and-white, sepia, or color, and if they should be printed. The very best photographers tend to get booked up many months in advance, so finding one is among the first tasks to attend to.

POESY RING

A band of gold inscribed on either the inside or outside with words of personal or sentimental meaning. Poesy rings were common during the Renaissance era and enjoyed popularity once again during the sentimental Victorian period.

An English book of 1624 entitled *Love's Garland, or, Posies for Rings, Handkerchiefs or Gloves and Such Pretty Tokens as Lovers Send their Loves* collected sentiments to be engraved on the inside of rings, including:

Amor vincit omnia (Love conquers all)

"I am yours"

"My love is true to none but you"

"In God and thee my joy shall be"

POSTURE

A bride's image is significantly influenced by how she stands and carries herself down the aisle. Good posture also enhances self-confidence and grace. While it is no longer necessary to refine posture by walking across a room balancing a pile of books on the head, a few lessons in deportment are still worth bearing in mind.

Harper's Bazaar, May 1952   "Poise is all important. A girl who habitually stoops and slouches will shuffle down the aisle: correct posture, therefore, is the first thing to cultivate."

Harper's Bazaar, May 1952 "The right way to stand is in a straight line from head to heel, chin and behind tucked in, ribs and chest drawn out of the self-controlled muscular girdle of taut mid-riff and held in stomach."

Vogue, April 1940 "Remember to walk with your chest up as you go up the aisle. Nothing will show off your small waist so well. Remember to hold your flowers low. Remember to take three deep breaths before you start—it will keep your knees from wobbling. Remember to 'lift your head behind your ears,' even if you are looking down; it accentuates that long slender-throated look."

POSEN, ZAC

American designer Zac Posen (b.1980) created a wonderfully unorthodox dress for his sister Alexandra's wedding in June 2004. Twenty craftsmen at Posen's studio worked into the night to cover the red gown's 6-foot (1.8-m) train with scarlet-and-fuchsia organza poppies.

POUF

Now used primarily to describe a puffball silhouette, "pouf" originally referred to an ornate headdress popular with women in the eighteenth century. French fashion designer Christian Lacroix (b.1951) is credited with introducing the *le pouf* dress, otherwise known as the puffball.

A "pouf" can also refer to the small burst of netting on a headband that some brides wear in preference to a traditional veil.

PRESSURE

Lady Georgiana Boothby (b.1947),
British PR consultant
"A single event with only one performance, no understudies, no retakes."

Vogue, April 1940
"As you walk down the aisle, your face misted in your white veil, which gives your skin an ethereal porcelain patina and your eyes a not strictly truthful depth and brilliance, you are setting yourself a standard of beauty which will take some effort to maintain."

Vogue, 1923
"There should be propaganda . . . against the nerve-wracking preparation for a fashionable wedding."

Vogue, April 1940
"To be content to remain forever imprinted on his heart as a photographic bride in cream satin, lace, and orchids is an impoverished ambition. His heart should be printed daily—like a newspaper."

PROCESSIONAL

The bride's journey down the aisle prior to the commencement of the wedding ceremony. Often she might hold her father's arm, with her bridesmaids following behind.

Vera Wang (b.1949),
American bridal wear designer
"The wedding processional represents the bride's most defining moment. After all the months of planning, a sense of anticipation is palpable as she begins her symbolic journey down the aisle."

is for QUEEN

QUEEN

Marianne Ostier (1902–76),
American jewelry designer

"There is one day on which every woman is queen; her bridal day—the day when all others yield place and do her deference. And she must remember that a queen always comports herself with dignity, yet is always gracious."

QUEEN VICTORIA

Queen Victoria instituted several fashions and customs concerning wedding style. Most important was the tradition of wearing a white wedding gown, which became established in Western culture upon her marriage to Prince Albert of Saxe-Coburg and Gotha in 1840. Victoria was also the first modern monarch to get married wearing a veil.

Her wedding gown was of white Spitalfields silk satin, trimmed with a flounce of Honiton lace, and she wore a matching lace veil. Queen Victoria ordered the veil personally from the lace-makers in the Devonshire village of Honiton as a gesture of her support for their trade, which was experiencing decline. The lace making was supervised by Miss Bidney, who employed more than two hundred workers to complete the commission between March and November 1839. To ensure that the lace would be unique, the patterns were destroyed after the dress was made.

Whereas Queen Victoria popularized many customs that have endured to the present day, she also rejected some established wedding traditions of the period. Rather than selecting the traditional plain wedding band, she chose a ring in the shape of a coiled serpent—the Ancient Egyptian symbol of eternity—with diamonds set in the place of the eyes.

is for RECEPTION

RECEPTION

It has long been expected that the wedding ceremony be followed by a reception, where the guests can eat and wish the newlyweds well in their married life, toast them with drinks and speeches, and celebrate the occasion with music and dancing. Until the late nineteenth century, Anglican weddings could only be solemnized between the hours of eight in the morning and midday, hence the term "wedding breakfast," which referred to the feasting that followed these early-morning unions. A Bill of 1886 extended the hours for wedding ceremonies until three in the afternoon. The change was met with general approbation, and in 1934, the hours were further extended to six in the evening.

Girl's Own Paper, 1886 "The wedding breakfast, which has been losing favour on account of its expense and its uselessness, will be entirely abolished; most weddings will be in the afternoon, the bridal party being an afternoon tea party instead, where tea and coffee and sandwiches and ices will be the heaviest 'eatables,' with the inevitable wedding cake, of course. A far pleasanter way of celebrating a marriage than the old wedding breakfast, which was generally dull beyond measure, and when it was over no one knew what to do with themselves for the rest of the day."

Vogue, May 1951 "Leave the ceremony to the church, where it beautifully belongs. But have a reception afterwards which is really a party—not a hallowed formula."

RECYCLE

Vogue, 1950s "The way to look at a wedding when you're the bride is as beautiful as your husband knows you are, as beautiful as you've always dreamed of being. The dress to crystallize that beauty, as timelessly right as in a Renaissance portrait, need not be expensive, or worn only once."

"The special wartime virtue of this model is that while it is every whit a wedding gown, it will be a perfectly practical dinner gown for the trousseau."

Not all brides want their dress to be a "once in a lifetime" gown, and a significant number opt for dresses that can be worn for other occasions. This is far from a new phenomenon. In fact, it was not until the 1960s that the notion of a "one-time" dress became entrenched. In the eighteenth and nineteenth centuries it was customary for most brides to be married in their best dresses, or to select a new gown that could be worn or altered for future use. In the 1920s, short, beaded chiffon or georgette chemise dresses were especially popular with working girls who could dye them afterward and wear them to dances. Many brides in the 1940s chose to marry in a smart suit, owing to the scarcity of luxury materials and the cost of weddings during wartime. In April 1955, *Harper's Bazaar* ran a "Wedding dresses with a future" feature, which promoted "a wedding dress which will transform itself, without the intervention of a dressmaker, into a beautiful dress for evening, or for a garden party."

DE LA RENTA, ÓSCAR
Óscar Arístides Ortiz de la Renta Fiallo (b.1932) is an award-winning Dominican fashion designer who specializes in red-carpet gowns, evening wear, and bridal wear. De la Renta became known in the 1960s for his couture designs for Jacqueline Kennedy. He was trained by Cristóbal Balenciaga and Antonio del Castillo and later worked for the houses of

Lanvin and Balmain. His own fashion house is a favorite among celebrities and royalty.

Óscar de la Renta (b.1932), Dominican fashion designer

"My designs are known for their beautiful ornamentation, details, fabrics, and embroideries, which are never more important than on a wedding dress."

RHODES, ZANDRA
Zandra Rhodes (b.1940) is a British fashion designer whose outrageous textile designs and punk creations helped put London at the forefront of the international fashion scene in the 1970s. Rhodes designed the wedding dress Elizabeth Weiner wore for her marriage to David Emanuel in 1976; the husband-and-wife design duo famously went on to design Princess Diana's wedding gown for her marriage.

In 1977 Rhodes designed a provocative punk wedding dress in silk jersey that was slashed to the thigh and across the leg and incorporated metallic chains that hung from the bodice and skirt.

RING (WEDDING)
Traditionally the wedding ring is a plain band without gemstones. The rationale for this is that by having no perceivable front or back designated by carvings or stones, the band encircles the finger in one unbroken line, echoing the eternity of the love and union it represents. Some brides, however, choose to have stones that complement their engagement ring set into their wedding rings.

While it has long been the custom for the groom to receive a wedding band, until the early twentieth century often only the bride received a ring during the wedding ceremony; additionally, it was not given that a groom would wear his ring all the time.

This practice changed after World War II, and the majority of men now wear wedding bands to complement those worn by their wives.

Vogue, February 1930

"The wide, thick, gold wedding band that grandma wore is as extinct as the dodo. The bride of today may choose a slim, gold circlet, but her preference is usually a fine plain or engraved platinum band, if a diamond ring is beyond the bridegroom's purse. The newest rings are of baguette diamonds set horizontally, or bands of clustered diamonds."

Marianne Ostier (1902–76), American jewelry designer

"In measuring the size of the wedding band, care should be taken not to make it too snug. Even if one is fortunate enough not to add weight with the years, the size of the fingers changes with the seasons. . . . It is better to fit the ring for the July finger, and in December, if necessary, wear an unobtrusive and attractive guard."

Wedding Etiquette, 1966

"The ring is made of gold to show how noble and durable are our affections; the form is round to imply that our regards shall never have an end, and the place is on the third finger of the left hand whence the ancients thought there was a vein which came directly from the heart."

Marianne Ostier (1902–76), American jewelry designer

"Two rings should not be worn at the same time on the same hand, except the wedding ring, which in due time comes to slide along the engagement ring to mark the fulfilment of the first ring's promise."

ROBE DE STYLE
A signature design of the Parisian couturier Jeanne Lanvin (1867–1946) in the 1920s. The *robe de style* dress was a popular style that offered an alternative to the straight-cut chemise; the bodice could be fitted or straight-cut in the chemise manner, with

a dropped waist, but it was characterized by its full skirts. The style was a popular choice among 1920s brides (see page 60).

Vogue, April 1925

"The *robe de style* is at its charming best for the average young girl. In fact, if you're still at all able to see yourself as the typical bride of romance, *Vogue* urges you not to consider any other kind of dress, for nothing is more picturesque, more lovely, when worn by the right type."

ROMANCE

Vogue, April 1921

"The white satin and old lace of a million romantic memories remain unrivaled for the wedding gown."

Vogue, April 1941

"[Here's t]o you . . . if you're romantic enough, if you're carrying flowers, to have a few sweetheart roses at the centre of your white bouquet; or to have there a few blue forget-me-nots, and for your bridesmaids, bunches of blue forget-me-nots tied with enormous pink bow pins."

Suzy Menkes (b.1943), British fashion journalist (on Princess Diana's wedding dress)

"Romance in cascades of silk. . . . The impression given as she stepped from her glass coach, with a full skirt below a tiny waist and the shimmering train snaking behind her, was of freshness and romance."

Edwina Ehrman (b.1953), British fashion curator

"The British taste for dressing up can be seen in the popularity of romantic wedding styles which draw on the cut, construction, and decorative details of historical dress."

Vera Wang (b.1949), American bridal wear designer

"The romanticist is transported by a dress. For her, fantasy is always a reality. Her innate femininity and love of beauty can inspire a gown of great fragility and enchantment."

ROYAL WEDDINGS

There is little that causes quite as much excitement as a royal wedding, and the promise of elaborate gowns of the finest craftsmanship and fabrics focuses all attention on the prospective royal bride. In Britain, people line the streets to catch a glimpse of the royal couple on their wedding day and share in the historic moment. The fact that royal weddings in Britain are broadcast across the globe cements the occasion as an elaborate celebration for the wider public to enjoy. Royal brides garner special interest and attention; the notion that they are on display to their public was epitomized by Queen Victoria's acquiescence to requests to wear her veil off her face so that she could be seen.

Queen Elizabeth, the Queen Mother

In 1923, Lady Elizabeth Bowes-Lyon married the Duke of York (later King George VI) in a gown of chiffon moiré. The dress had a deep, square neckline with a narrow piped edge and sleeves that were trimmed similarly. It was a very simple design, with a bodice cut straight to the waist, without darts. The back extended to form a separate train. A *Point de Flandres* lace veil, lent to her by Queen Mary, was worn low on her forehead, which was the fashion of the times, and held in place by a band of myrtle leaves and two white roses and orange blossoms over each ear. She was the last British royal bride to wear flowers in her hair.

The Times, April 26, 1923

"The simplest dress ever made for a royal wedding."

Queen Elizabeth II

British couturier Sir Norman Hartnell (1901–79) was appointed to design Princess Elizabeth's dress for her marriage to Prince Philip in 1947. The gown, which was loosely based on the figure of Flora in Sandro Botticelli's *La Primavera* (c.1482), was a vision of romantic elegance, featuring an eminently feminine sweetheart neckline and a fashionable full skirt with soft folds of satin. Hartnell was renowned for his love of embellishment, and the gown and

18-foot (5.5-m) train were richly embroidered with more than ten thousand seed pearls and thousands of white beads. The decorative scheme incorporated traditional floral motifs, including roses, orange blossom, and sprays of corn. Princess Elizabeth was not exempt from wartime clothing restrictions, and, like many brides of the 1940s, she had to pay for the ensemble's fabric with her ration coupons.

Sir Norman Hartnell (1901–79) also designed the wedding gown for the queen's sister, Princess Margaret, who married the photographer Antony Armstrong-Jones in May 1960. The white silk organza gown, an unusually simple design for Hartnell, suited the princess's taste and was remarkably effective. The unfussiness of the dress, whose upper layer comprised 90 feet (27 m) of diaphanous silk, allowed for some statement accessories, including a diamond necklace of Margaret's grandmother, Queen Mary, and the large Poltimore Tiara.

"It seems as though she moved in a soft white cloud."

Arguably the most memorable royal bride of the twentieth century, Princess Diana married Prince Charles in a lavish ceremony at St. Paul's Cathedral in July 1981. Her gown, with its voluminous full skirt and puffed sleeves of ivory silk taffeta and antique lace, as well as a 25-foot (7.6-m) detachable court train, reinstated a trend for the quintessential romantic wedding dress. It was ornamented with hand embroidery, sequins, and more than ten thousand pearls.

The first copy of the dress reputedly arrived in a Debenhams' shop window just five hours after the ceremony took place.

"Diana was not just a bride; she was *the* bride."

"The romantic ruffle that the Princess of Wales has made her fashion hallmark was the focal point of her fairy-tale wedding dress."

is for SILHOUETTE

SCENT

A person's choice of fragrance acts as a signature
that can be just as powerful an identifier as
their physical features. Scent is evocative and
provocative, conjuring up images of an individual
and, therefore, particular moments and places.
Scents can be light and floral, heady and mature,
and everything in between. Some people like to
experiment with different fragrances, while others
stay loyal to one scent.

Vogue, May 1985	"Fragrance first. . . . It's not only the first fashion a woman wears, but the key to a first impression."
Harper's Bazaar, May 1952	"Your scent should be light and sweet or delicate and gay."
Harper's Bazaar, May 1952	"For a fair bride: Chanel no. 22 or Atkinson's *Bal des Fleurs*. For a dark bride: Patou's *L'Heure Attendue* or Floris English Lilac. For a red-haired bride: Caron's *Fleurs de Rocaille* or Lenthéric's *Confetti*."
Jennifer Aniston (b.1969), American actress	"One tradition I have with my friends is that when one of us gets married, we have a ton of fragrance oils and pretty bottles at a bachelorette party. Everyone puts a drop or two in a bottle for the bride and makes a wish, and the bride wears our creation on her wedding day."
Vogue, May 1985	"Fragrance. . . . The provocative element of style. Romantically inclined. The possibilities abound."

SECOND-TIME BRIDES

Divorce and remarriage are no longer a taboo but a
reality of modern life. Second marriages are equally

legitimate expressions of true love, and they deserve the recognition and celebration that first weddings garner.

Vera Wang (b.1949), American bridal wear designer

"Marriage in whatever form, and at whatever stage in life, symbolizes the coming together of two souls who have found each other."

SHOES

Although elegant footwear has always been considered a staple of the bridal ensemble, it was not until bridal hemlines rose above the ankle in the 1920s that wedding shoes garnered special significance, and designers and manufacturers began to create more innovative designs. Much attention was paid to the style of the heel. The "Louis" heel, which had enjoyed popularity since the turn of the century, endured as a fashionable choice, but thick "Cuban" and slender "spike" heels were other favorites.

For the most part, bridal footwear is feminine and elegant. Soft leathers and designs overlaid with cream silk or satin fabrics, or embellished with details such as bows, buckles, and paste jewels, remain common choices. Some brides regard their wedding day as the perfect reason to indulge in a pair of designer, statement heels and spend a significant sum on their wedding shoes, rationalizing that they will be worn again.

Vogue, May 1918

"In accordance with the custom of her grandmother, white satin slippers carry the bride on her adventurous voyage down the aisle into matrimony. But today's slippers show a rosette of white chiffon with a centre of orange-blossoms to peep below her satin skirt."

Harper's Bazaar, February 1965

"Wedding gaiety goes deep down to elegant feet beneath ankle-length dresses."

Marlene Dietrich (1901–92),
German-born
American actress

"Shoes are more important than good suits and dresses. Good shoes give elegance to your entire appearance."

The Complete Guide to
Wedding Etiquette, 1960

"Satin or crêpe slippers should be worn, and should match the wedding gown. Toeless sandals should not be worn. Pumps may be decorated with a lace bow and sandals should be plain."

SHOWER

A bridal shower is a gathering of the bride's closest friends before the wedding day wherein she can enjoy the company of her friends and reaffirm the bonds of friendship before marriage; it is an established American custom now gaining popularity in Britain. Bridal showers also give married friends and family members an opportunity to impart their wisdom regarding married life to the bride.

The term "shower" was coined by a society column in an American newspaper in the early 1800s, when a reporter described how the bride's friends had placed wrapped gifts in an inverted Japanese parasol, which, when turned upside down, "showered" upon the bride. The word soon became common parlance, and the umbrella remains a symbol of the bridal shower.

SILHOUETTE

The shape and outline of someone or something visible against a lighter background.

The modern bride is confronted with an abundance of styles and silhouettes for her wedding gown. Some brides-to-be opt for tradition and select princess or full-length A-line gowns that have enjoyed popularity throughout the twentieth and twenty-first centuries; others are drawn to particular historical styles, such as Empire-line gowns or the sleek sheath dresses of the 1930s; a smaller number wish to keep apace with contemporary developments in fashion and select a design or design features that are currently in vogue.

Jenny Packham (b.1965), British fashion designer

"A lot of people say, 'I want a dress that I'm going to be happy looking at in ten years. I don't want it to look dated.' But the bad news is it will. So just live in the moment and choose something that suits you."

Ballerina

Ballerina dresses are usually strapless and feature a close-fitting bodice and a full skirt that falls to the calf, thereby exposing the lower leg and ankles. They are considered youthful and dainty and are best constructed from layers of tulle, owing to its frothy qualities.

Harper's Bazaar, May 1952

"The newest, youngest bridal dress, charming for any, but great for traditional weddings, is short; it clears the ground, ballerina-length, or even just covering the calf."

Empire line

The Empire line was the fashionable silhouette in early nineteenth-century France and especially during the First Empire (1804–15), which followed the turbulent years of the French Revolution. The style was also popular during the corresponding Regency period in England (1811–20). Empire-line dresses feature a high waist with a seam tucked just under the bust, and a long, columnar skirt. The style

Ballerina   *Empire line*   *Princess line*

emphasizes the bust and a low décolleté. Empire-line dresses have enjoyed recurring popularity as a choice for bridal wear because of their eminently simple design. Elbow-length gloves look particularly elegant with the Empire style.

Princess line

Princess-line dresses feature a full skirt and a close-fitting bodice cut in linear panels so that there is no waist seam interrupting it from the skirt. The British couturier Charles Frederick Worth (1825–95) is credited with having invented the style in the 1860s for a dress he designed for the Empress Eugenie. Its lack of waist seam makes it flattering to most figures. It enjoyed particular popularity during the 1960s and 1970s.

Heavier fabrics such as duchess satin, silk brocades, and corded silks are required, as the dress needs to have a certain amount of weight and body to hold the flared shape of the skirt.

Riding habit

The equestrian style, which takes as its inspiration the fitted jackets and full skirts worn by women for horseback-riding in the nineteenth century, offers an alternative silhouette for the bride who does not wish to wear lace and ruffles on her wedding day. The riding habit typically consists of a jacket that is fitted at the waist and flares out to form either a peplum or tails. The classic gigot, or leg-of-mutton, sleeves that puff at the shoulder and taper to fit closely at the wrist are also characteristic of the style, which enjoyed renewed popularity in the 1990s.

Riding habit

Romantic (see overleaf)

Sheath (see overleaf)

Romantic	The "romantic" wedding gown remains one of the most popular styles for wedding dresses, featuring a fitted bodice, full skirt, and train at the back.
	One of the most memorable wedding dresses in the romantic style was the gown designed by the Emanuels for Princess Diana's wedding to the Prince of Wales in July 1981.
Catherine Woram (b.1964), British author on wedding dress style	"Far-removed from the ordinary everyday dress, this enchanting style recalls another era and is part of the fairytale portrayal of weddings that we see in films and read in literature throughout our lives."
Sheath	Floor-length gowns that are loose fitting and skim the curves of the body. The silhouette is associated with the shiny, seductive gowns worn by Hollywood stars in the 1930s. Sheath dresses can fall straight to the floor or incorporate a small, circular train. Mermaid dresses are a variation of the sheath dress and taper in at the knee before gently flaring to the floor, creating the effect of a mermaid's tail.

SIMPLICITY

Madeleine Ginsburg (b.1928), British fashion curator	"It is because of their apparent simplicity that modern wedding dresses are so demanding in the requirements that they make of the designer."
Giorgio Armani (b.1934), Italian fashion designer	"The essence of style is a simple way of saying something complex."
Edith Head (1897–1981), American costume designer	"Simplification is the best medicine for making a beautiful woman more beautiful."
The Times, March 29, 1920	"Many of the modern wedding dresses incline to a greater simplicity than French custom has hitherto sanctioned. . . ."
Vogue, June 1998	"The frill is gone: taking a vow of simplicity requires stripping away all extravagance."

Vera Wang (b.1949), American bridal wear designer

"The simpler the gown, the more precise the workmanship should be."

SKIRTS

The skirts of bridal gowns can be long, short, wide, narrow, or anywhere in between. Some of the most popular styles are:

A-line (see page 9) A skirt that is either narrow or fitted at the hips and flares gently to a widened hemline.

Asymmetrical A skirt with a graduated hemline; typically calf length at the front and falling to the floor at the rear.

Balloon (pouf) Usually short, a balloon skirt is a full, gathered shape that tapers at the hemline.

Columnar A floor-length skirt that forms a close-fitting sheath over the body.

Full An enormous, gathered skirt. The full skirt is particularly suited to formal or traditional weddings and connotes grandeur.

Mermaid A close-fitting, floor-length skirt that accentuates the curves of the body by tapering to the knee before flaring gently to the floor.

SOMETHING OLD, SOMETHING NEW...

A nineteenth-century wedding rhyme relating to the bride's attire. Incorporating the elements of old, new, borrowed, and blue in the bride's wedding attire was supposed to ensure happiness and prosperity in her married life. Many brides still choose to adopt the tradition today.

Something old,
Something new,
Something borrowed,
Something blue,
and a silver sixpence in her shoe.
—*Nineteenth-century wedding rhyme*

Vogue, April 1941 "Have your initials embroidered in pale blue (that 'something blue') on your long white wedding gloves."

According to a *Daily Mail* survey, two-thirds of 1960s brides paid attention to the tradition on their wedding day, compared to just 39 percent of brides who wed in the years 2000–10.

STRAPLESS

Many brides opt for a strapless dress, but despite their popularity, the style can be unflattering on many figures.

Jenny Packham (b.1965), British fashion designer

"I feel like maybe the sort of strapless, big dress has maybe had its day."

Vera Wang (b.1949), American bridal wear designer

"Bare, yet refined, romantic, but dignified, a strapless neckline strikes the perfect balance between propriety and flirtation."

Kristie Lau, Australian fashion journalist

"With the exception of a lucky few, most wearers risk spillover cleavage, skin bunching beneath the arms and the dreaded uniboob."

SUPERSTITIONS

Married in white,
She has chosen all right.
Married in blue,
Her love will be true.
Married in yellow,
She'll be ashamed of her fellow.
Married in red,
She'll wish herself dead.
Married in black,
She'll wish herself back.

Married in gray,
She'll travel far away.
Married in pink,
And her spirits will sink.
Married in green,
She'll be ashamed to be seen.
—*Wedding proverb*

Married in January's frost and rime,
Widows you'll be before your time.
Married in February's cruel weather,
Life you'll walk in tune together.
Married when March winds blow and roar,
Your home will be on some foreign shore.
Married 'neath April's changeful skies,
A checkered path before you lies.
Married in May when honey bees flit,
Strangers around your table will sit.
Married during the month of June,
Life will be one long honeymoon.
Married in July when the flowers are ablaze,
Bittersweet memories in after days.
Married in August's heat and drowse,
Lover and friend in your chosen spouse.
Married in September's autumn glow,
Smooth and serene your life will flow.
Married when October leaves grow thin,
Toil and hardship for both begin.
Married in November's month of list,
Fortune your wedding ring has kissed.
When December's snow falls fast,
The marriage is happy and love will last.
—*Wedding proverb*

is for TIARA

TASTE

Taste is a sociological construct that epitomizes a delicacy of style that is conditioned by one's sensitivity and responses to artistic and aesthetic matters, including architecture, fine art, and literature. Taste also entails making judgments about the styles individuals adopt in matters such as their personal appearance, possessions, and residential interiors.

Vera Wang (b.1949), American bridal wear designer

"When you're talking about a wedding, it's a fine line between fantasy and good taste."

TEARS

The Etiquette of Marriage, 1857

"The bride may have her brow decorated with sparkling and costly pearls, but these are often accompanied by the pearly tears bedewing her eye-lashes, and trickling down her lovely cheeks."

The Ladies' Treasury, 1858

GERALDINE: "[My veil] shall cover my head, face, and, as far as possible, my person; and I shall have it very thickly flowered, that no one may see the tears I know will gush forth when I think I am leaving you."

MRS VERNON: "Nor the happy blushes that will suffuse your cheeks when you remember that you are leaving me for him."

TIARA

A crownlike ornament or headdress, which is often set with stones and worn by brides or as an article of formal dress.

Vera Wang (b.1949), American bridal wear designer

"A tiara can be positively magical. However, it requires enormous personal style to wear a tiara effectively."

Geoffrey Munn (b.1953),
British jewelry historian
and author

"The tiara, the most elegant and dramatic of all jewels, has the unique ability to make a bride feel and look the centre of attention. It is the endorsement of her status as queen of the day."

TOP HAT AND TAILS

A formal menswear ensemble, consisting of a tall, cylindrical hat, usually of felt or beaver, and a dress coat cut at the back to hang to the mid-calf in two "tails." A top hat and tails is traditionally worn with a dress shirt, waistcoat, and trousers and remains a popular choice of dress for the groom and the father of the bride.

The vogue for wearing formal, tailored menswear, such as frock coats and morning coats, at weddings is particularly British. Tailoring continues to endure as a particular strength among British designers.

TRAIN

A trailing part of a gown or dress, lengthened so that it drapes along the ground—although in many cases it is held by attendants. Alternatively made from a piece of cloth attached to the dress.

Although many nineteenth-century evening and bridal gowns incorporated a train of fabric that extended from the back, it was not until the 1870s that separate trains of material began to be attached at the shoulders or waist.

Royal brides are renowned for their elaborate trains. Queen Victoria's bridal ensemble included an 18-foot (5.5-m) train of satin and lace. Princess Diana's comprised 25 feet (7.6 m) of sweeping satin.

LENGTHS OF WEDDING
DRESS TRAINS

Brush   The shortest style of train, which "brushes" the ground behind the dress to add a modest amount of volume to the gown. They are extremely versatile and practical to wear.

Court   Court trains extend approximately 3 feet (1 m) behind the waist. They are not a practical choice for weddings conducted on grass or sand.

Chapel   A stylish compromise between the simplicity of the Brush and Court trains, and the formality of the Cathedral and Royal trains, chapel-length trains extend approximately 6 to 7 feet (2 m) from the waist.

Cathedral   Most suited to formal, traditional weddings, Cathedral-length trains make a bold statement, since they extend 9 feet (3 m) from the waist. They require assistance to keep them in order.

Royal   A train extending 26 feet (8 m) from the waist to span the aisle of the church or cathedral. Royal trains are traditionally reserved for only the grandest and most formal wedding ceremonies and require several attendants to maneuver.

Watteau   A single panel of fabric that attaches, often in gathers, to the top of the dress, either at the shoulders or upper back of the bodice. Watteau trains can be of the same length as the gown and fall straight to the ground, or they can extend out at the back to create a more dramatic look.

TRIMMINGS

Decorative articles, often of ribbon, lace, or other fabric, that are attached to a garment to enhance its ornamental qualities.

Eschelles	Rows of ribbon bows, diminishing in size, which are sewn down the center of the bodice or stomacher (dress panel).
Passementerie	Decorative and often sumptuous trimming consisting of braids, tassels, gimps, etc., variously made from silk, linen, wool, cotton, and silver and gold thread, etc., and originally popularized by French designs in the seventeenth century.
Ribbon	A narrow strip of fabric, used either as a binding or tie or for purely ornamental purposes as a decorative accessory. Ribbons are often corded at both edges to prevent fraying and are made from a variety of fabrics, including satin, organza, silk, grosgrain, and velvet.
Rosette	A rose-shaped arrangement of ribbons often attached to items of dress as a decorative ornament.
Ruffle	A ruffle—also known as a frill or furbelow—is a strip of fabric, lace, or ribbon that is gathered and pleated on one edge and attached to a garment or accessory as a type of trimming.
Halston (1932–90), American fashion designer	"I like the idea that a ruffle seems to come from nothing. I like things that are sculptural and yet are soft."
Sash	A length of fabric worn over one shoulder, as in ceremonial regalia, or around the waist.

TROUSSEAU

From the French *truss*, meaning "little bundle." The trousseau refers to the clothes a woman takes on her honeymoon, and traditionally in preparation for her first year of married life. In the past this included lingerie, daywear, evening gowns for balls and other social commitments, shoes, stockings, and accessories such as gloves, scarves, and hair ornaments.

I Do! I Do! From the Veil to the Vows, Susan Waggoner, 2002	"The trousseau was the last grand fashion splurge for the bride-to-be before the transition from carefree girl to care-burdened wife."
Vogue, May 1914	"To buy enough, yet not too much, to resist the wiles of the *Couturier and Modiste*, and yet to provide clothes for every occasion for every possible emergency is the difficult problem of the bride."
Vogue, April 1940	"A vital and fundamental part of the wedding trousseau is your shoe wardrobe."
Vogue, April 1919	"Lacy sheerness and pale colors find their soft insidious ways to win a very important place in the bride's trousseau."
Vogue, May 1918	"A trousseau without a silk afternoon frock is a trousseau that is but half-prepared for the emergencies of married life."
The Complete Guide to Wedding Etiquette, 1960	"The modern plan is to have only what is necessary to carry the bride through the first year of married life."
	"It must be emphasized that in selecting her trousseau, the bride should exercise taste and discretion. Each article should be as good as she can afford, and suited to her circumstances. The bride should mark all her trousseau clothes with her married initials or name."
Vogue, September 1922	"In our grandmother's day, the romantic halo of engagement might rest for years above a maiden brow, while the maiden in question collected a trousseau and a store of sentimental impressions, both sufficient to last a lifetime."

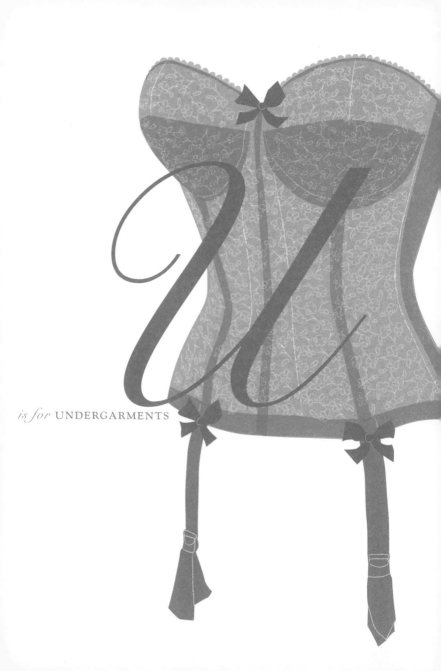

is for UNDERGARMENTS

UNDERGARMENTS

Many wedding dresses require a particular type of undergarment to achieve the desired silhouette. Although many brides view their wedding as an opportunity to indulge in special, fine lingerie, thought needs to be given to whether the desired underwear is appropriate for the dress that will be worn over it. A red lace basque (corset) is not a suitable base for a sheath dress of silk chiffon. As many wedding gowns are selected without regard for the season, thermal or silk and wool-mix underwear can be a savvy choice for the winter bride. Some pretty styles of thermal underwear are now available, trimmed with lace. "Sensible" does not have to mean "unattractive."

USHER

The principal duty of ushers is to direct people to their seats and to ensure that everyone is seated in advance of the start of the ceremony. Often ushers are close friends of the groom, or sometimes younger male relatives of the bride. Today only the most formal weddings are conducted in accordance with a seating plan, meaning the role of the usher is more of an acknowledgment of the man's close association to the bride and groom than an established set of duties.

Esquire Fashion Guide for All Occasions, 1957

"It is customary for ushers to pay extra attention to unescorted ladies in showing them to their seats. . . . At the reception they attend unescorted ladies and mingle generally with the guests."

"Manner should be friendly and cordial. Welcoming, but no prolonged contact."

is for VEIL

VEIL

Veils form the oldest part of the wedding ensemble and predate the formal wedding gown by at least a thousand years. The concealment of a bride's face behind a veil is symbolic of her being delivered to her groom as a pure and innocent maiden. Superstition held that the veil also protected the bride from evil spirits who might wish to thwart her happiness.

Veils have fluctuated in popularity over the centuries. Many Elizabethan brides selected Juliet caps trimmed with lace and embroidery instead, and in the eighteenth century, bonnets, caps, wreaths, and tiaras were popular alternatives. The preference for wearing a veil became reestablished during the nineteenth century—in part due to Queen Victoria's electing to wear one for her 1840 marriage to Prince Albert. The trend was also a product of advances in technology that meant that tulle, traditionally a staple component of the veil, could be produced in greater widths and quantities, which made it an affordable option to a greater number of brides.

Vogue, May 1916

"There could be nothing new in the wedding ceremony; there could be nothing particularly new about the groom; so on the bride's head be it—all the novelty was concentrated in the wedding veil."

Harper's Bazaar, February 1965

"Veils no longer hide elated faces and are transformed into ornament in shapely bridal hair."

Mary Brooks Picken (1886–1981), American fashion writer

"Veils, like perfume, are an exquisite luxury if they are dainty, delicate, and becoming."

Vogue, April 1920

"Such is the texture of a bridal veil, fluffs of fairy moonshine, misty, trailing; partly fashioned of the stuff of happiness and partly of some rare old lace or tulle."

Vogue, May 1918

"A cloud of tulle held to the head with a diamond band; a veil of Limerick lace patterned like a faint shadow, caught at the back with orange blossoms. . . ."

VEIL STYLES

Petal (cage)

Petal veils are either short and slightly gathered, or flat and circular, and are split down the front at the center with a square or rounded edge.

Circular (dropped)

A flat, ungathered piece of tulle that is dropped on the head and secured with a comb and hairpins. Veils of this type create volume but no height.

Mantilla

Of Spanish origin; a lace, draped veil that sits over the hair falling around the face.

VEIL LENGTHS

Shoulder

Among the shortest types; typically 20 inches (50 cm) long.

Elbow

Falls at the body near the elbow; typically 25 inches (65 cm).

Waist

Intended to fall to the natural waist; approximately 30 inches (80 cm) long.

Fingertip

Typically a 44-inch (110-cm) train.

Ballet

Sometimes called a waltz veil, a ballet veil falls somewhere between the knees and the calves; approximately 56 inches (150 cm) long.

Floor

Extends all the way to the ground; the standard length for a floor-length veil is 108 inches (275 cm).

Chapel

Typically worn for church weddings and by brides wishing to create a dramatic entrance; cut to finish with gown's train.

Cathedral

Usually reserved for the most formal church weddings; a veil of 144 inches (365 cm).

Veils can comprise single or multiple tiers and can be trimmed with lace or ribbon and embellished with decorative details such as sequins and pearls.

VINTAGE

Vera Wang (b.1949),
American bridal wear designer

"Since vintage dresses are one of a kind, they can be perfect for the bride who desires something truly unique."

The appeal of a vintage wedding dress endures among many modern brides-to-be, especially for those who are interested in historical styles. There is also something romantic about a wedding dress with a history that appeals to brides with sentimental tendencies. Vintage wedding dresses can be difficult and costly to alter, however, because often the materials they are made of are no longer available, and it can be time-consuming and expensive to source suitable alternatives.

Vintage cars, such as a classic Rolls-Royce, remain popular among couples wishing to leave the wedding venue for the reception or their honeymoon in style.

VIRGINAL

French fashion designer Christian Lacroix (b.1951) designed an embroidered silk dress for his 1993–94 Autumn/Winter collection entitled *Qui a le droit? (Who has the right?)*. The design, and title, invited comment about whether it is appropriate for a contemporary bride to wear a wedding dress in a color associated with purity and chastity.

Sophie Ellis-Bextor (b.1979),
British singer

"On my wedding day I didn't want a natural, blushing-bride look—I had a full-on hairdo and red lips. I thought it would be disingenuous to do the whole virginal look, so even though I had the white dress, I had pink net underneath."

VOGUE

Since its inception in 1892, *Vogue* magazine has been instrumental in promoting the latest bridal fashions and designs through its publications in America, France, Britain, and a host of other countries. The magazine continues to play an important role in guiding brides-to-be toward the bridal shops and services that are most useful to them, as well as giving its advice and opinions on designers and the latest fashionable styles, fabrics, and accessories.

Vogue also influenced brides' sartorial choices through the many sewing patterns it promoted. The magazine included a sewing pattern as early as 1899, but it wasn't until the 1940s that the feature expanded to become *Vogue Patterns*, a separate entity that introduced haute couture patterns and the latest bridal designs into the realm of home dressmaking. These patterns were especially popular in the 1940s and 1950s, when women frequently made many of their own clothes.

VOWS

The vows are the promise of lasting commitment that couples make to one another during the wedding. The wording of the vows varies according to the ceremony, and—in the case of religious services—may depend on the faith and denomination of the couple. Couples married in secular ceremonies often personalize their vows, and many couples choose to write their own.

A. A. Milne (1882–1956), children's author

"If you live to be a hundred, I hope I live to be a hundred minus one day, so I never have to live without you."

is for WREATH

WANG, VERA

Vera Wang (b.1949) is an award-winning American fashion and bridal wear designer and former senior fashion editor of *Vogue*. Wang left her post as design director of Ralph Lauren in 1990 to establish her own bridal boutique, and her name is now synonymous with wedding style. She has designed gowns for a host of high-profile clients, including Chelsea Clinton, Mariah Carey, Victoria Beckham, Kate Hudson, and Kim Kardashian. The character Charlotte York in the television series *Sex and the City* declared a Vera Wang gown to be the "perfect" dress for her wedding to Trey MacDougal.

Vera Wang (b.1949), American bridal wear designer

"There was no relationship between a wedding dress and fashion. There was no good taste, either. I realized that I could make an impression in terms of changing and readdressing the whole industry of bridal."

WARTIME BRIDES

The traditional white wedding gown proved an unattainable dream for many brides during the years of World War I and World War II. The British Board of Trade introduced a series of measures controlling the supply of cloth, clothing, and footwear to address the problems of materials shortages and the consequential rising costs. Two measures were the Utility Scheme (1941), which granted all civilians a supply of coupons for articles of food and clothing to ensure a fairer distribution to all, and Civilian Clothing Orders (1942), which imposed stringent regulations governing the construction, materials, and trimming of nearly every item of clothing, including wedding dresses.

The restrictions applied to all clothing, be it made by a couture fashion house or a factory.

People could still use their coupons to buy fabric for weddings dresses, such as man-made satins, but such fabrics would require many coupons and so were deemed too frivolous for some. Many, therefore, opted to wear two-piece suits, which they would be able to wear again.

Dresses produced in line with the Civilian Clothing restrictions carried the cc41 utility clothing mark and were named "Utility Wedding Dresses." Such garments abided by restrictions governing aspects such as the length of the hemline and the level of surface detail and ornamentation, and they tended to make sparing use of material. Clever designers were able to add individuality to their garments through innovative cuts and seams and by paying close attention to smaller details such as buttonholes and lapels.

Eleanor Roosevelt, First Lady of the United States during World War II, organized a group of society ladies in America to donate wedding dresses to brides of British servicemen. What became known as the "Roosevelt dress" was a Tudor-style, lavish design in heavily embossed cream brocade. It incorporated a circular train and was accompanied by a silk veil, held in place by a Juliet cap and wreath of flowers.

WAX FLOWERS

Delicate, artificial flowers made from wax, or sometimes paper and wax, which are wired onto a band to form a headdress or wreath, or arranged into a spray to form a corsage or other floral arrangement. Wax flowers were especially fashionable among Victorian brides when the craft of wax-flower making was a popular hobby for women. Many brides preferred wax or other artificial flowers to real ones, as they could be kept as a memento of the wedding day.

WESTWOOD, VIVIENNE

Dame Vivienne Westwood DBE (Daughters of the British Empire) (b.1941) is a British fashion designer credited with having brought punk fashions into the mainstream. She is an established name in couture and ready-to-wear designs and a favorite among celebrities. Westwood, who launched her first bridal collection for Liberty of London in January 1993, is known for her extravagant and sumptuous approach to bridal wear. Her designs typically feature full skirts that billow over layers of underskirts and her signature built-in corsets, inspired by eighteenth-century fashions. Carrie Bradshaw wore a Westwood gown in champagne silk before she was jilted by Big in the film based on the HBO television series *Sex and the City*, and the dress piqued the fantasies of many brides-to-be. Netaporter.com soon launched a cocktail-length version of the dress costing $7,760, and it sold out within hours of release. The original full-length gown is available made-to-order from Vivienne Westwood; prices start at $18,860.

WHITE

The classic white wedding gown endures for many as the quintessential element of bridal attire. Queen Victoria established the vogue for wearing the color when she married Prince Albert of Saxe-Coburg and Gotha in 1840, and since then white has persisted as a popular choice for wedding gowns—because of its association with the qualities of purity, innocence, and virginity. Whereas the acceptance of "virgin white" as the prevailing color for a wedding dress coincided with an age of sentiment and Victorian morality, a large number of modern women no longer feel comfortable with these associations. Many believe that to walk down the aisle as a picture of virginal innocence would be disingenuous. While some are keen to abide by tradition and marry in classic white, just as many prefer to select either shades of cream, ivory, or oyster, or to opt for bold colors such as red or blue.

American bridal wear designer Vera Wang (b.1949) advises brides who do decide upon a white gown to choose a shade that complements their skin tone. Pure and brilliant whites can flatter rosy complexions, while warmer tones tend to look most flattering on darker skin. In grayer winter light, ivories and off-whites cast an air of sophistication over the gown and bride.

Vogue, April 1921 — "After several centuries of custom, a wedding without a gown of white satin and old lace is hardly legal."

Vera Wang (b.1949), American bridal wear designer — "White implies weddings. From the iciest shades of blue-white to the warmth and luxury of ivory, white remains an incredible source of inspiration."

To Have and to Hold: 135 Years of Wedding Fashions, Charles L. Mo, 2000 — "Perhaps no garment better symbolizes one of life's special moments than does a white wedding gown and the focus it brings to the bride during the wedding ceremony."

Madeleine Ginsburg (b.1928), British fashion curator — "The formal 'white' wedding gown is, by definition, confined to a limited range of color and depends on contrasts of texture and nuances of tone for its decorative effect."

Edwina Ehrman (b.1953), British fashion curator — "The marriage of Queen Victoria to Prince Albert of Saxe-Coburg and Gotha on 10 February 1840 was a defining moment in the history of the white wedding dress in Britain."

Vera Wang (b.1949), American bridal wear designer

"The marriage of different whites provides depth, dimension and texture without the distraction of color."

WIDOW

Manners and Rules of Good Society or Solecisms to be Avoided, 1902

"A bride who is a widow should not wear white, nor a bridal veil, nor a wreath of orange blossoms, nor orange blossoms on her dress. She should not be attended by bridesmaids, and wedding favors should not be worn by the guests."

Vogue, October 1936

"When a widow or a divorced woman remarries, invitations or announcements are sent out exactly as at her first marriage, except that her married surname is included. . . . The bride never wears white, but usually wears an afternoon dress and hat in a light, becoming color. The fact that the bridegroom has been married before does not alter the wedding in any respect."

WREATH

An arrangement of real or artificial flowers and foliage on a wired, circular band. Wreaths can be worn in the hair as headdresses, but they might also be used as ornaments to decorate doors or tables.

The Ladies' Treasury, 1858

"Your wreath or your hair must be so arranged, that the veil may drop gracefully from it, not rub (as Emily Murray's did) against your nose; her wreath was placed at the back of her head (alone), a very great mistake, and the tip of her nose was so grazed by the friction of the lace, that it was quite red and made her look a very great fright at her wedding breakfast."

is for X-TREME

X-RATED BRIDAL WEAR

Some celebrities have caused a sensation with their bridal wear. When Bianca Pérez-Mora Macias married Rolling Stones frontman Mick Jagger in 1971, she opted for a white Yves Saint Laurent Le Smoking jacket, wearing nothing underneath; in 2006 model and actress Pamela Anderson caused a minor sensation when she married Kid Rock in a white string bikini.

Kristen McMenamy (b.1966), American model

"I wanted to look naked for my wedding. So I asked Karl [Lagerfeld] to design me a dress that gave the illusion of naked flesh, without being naked."

Bridal style doesn't have to be confined to the wedding day. Model Chrissy Teigen has recently designed a line of bridal bikinis and swimwear for Beach Bunny Swimwear, perfect for beach-based honeymoons. The designs are predominantly white and feature details such as Swarovski crystals, Chantilly lace, and the word *Bride* across the bottoms.

X-TREME

Some brides more than others aspire to make a statement and stand out on their wedding day. An Italian bride set a new world record in September 2011 when she married in the city of Naples wearing a veil that was 1.75 miles (3 km) long.

is for YOUTHFUL

YOUTHFUL

Wedding dresses of the 1910s were youthful in style and appearance, with their characteristic shorter, ankle-length skirts that revealed white satin slippers.

Vogue, May 1914 — "There is no denying that the short skirt and short veil make the average bride look at least three years younger than she is."

Vogue, May 1916 — "When the bride's mother wears this gown, the guests murmur, 'But my dear, she looks young enough to be the bride's sister.' It is [a Worth dress] of silk striped blue and grey, with a bodice of grey chiffon and silver lace over mauve silk."

Marianne Ostier (1902–76), American jewelry designer — "There may perhaps also be in her costume the suggestion that, mother though she is, she still possesses freshness, vitality, and youth."

is for ZZZZ . . .

ZZZZ . . .

It is estimated that slightly more than half of
newlywed couples do not consummate their
marriage on the wedding night. Reasons for this
include tiredness, arguing before the end of the
reception, and consuming too much alcohol. Many
couples no longer leave the wedding reception early,
instead choosing to party into the night with their
guests. Those concerned about succumbing to this
statistic should perhaps reserve their special lingerie
for the honeymoon instead.

ACKNOWLEDGMENTS

I wish to thank all my colleagues in the Furniture, Textiles and Fashion Department, but especially Jenny Lister for giving me the opportunity to write this book, and Edwina Ehrman for suggesting the entry on "Tears" and for supplying the perfect quote. I am also grateful to two talented interns, Susanna Cordner and Charlotte Quinn, for helping to locate facts and fill gaps.

I would like to thank Davina Cheung, Clare Davis, Mark Eastment, Sally Griffiths, Reena Kataria, and Tom Windross of V&A Publishing. My thanks also go to copy editor Rebeka Russell for her thoughtful suggestions.

As always, I thank my immensely supportive parents, Julia and Peter, and my best friends Lauren, Rachel, Laura, Jo, and Jaron for their constant encouragement and belief in me.

REFERENCES

Classic style guides are cited by book title; named authors and quoted texts by author; websites are cited where the taken quotation is exclusive to them.

INTRODUCTION
PAGE 6: Blanche Ebbutt, *Don'ts for Wives* (London 1913), p.v

A
See further, Catherine Woram, *Wedding Dress Style* (London 1993); PAGE 9: Christian Dior cited in Amy de la Haye, *A–Z of Style* (London 2011), p.11; PAGE 10: *The Etiquette of Marriage* (Halifax 1857), p.25; PAGE 11: Stephen Jones cited from queensofvintage.com (accessed July 26, 2013); Alison Adburgham cited in Amy de la Haye, *A–Z of Style* (London 2011), p.83

B
See further, Susan Waggoner, *I Do! I Do! From the Veil to the Vows: How Classic Wedding Traditions Came to Be* (New York 2002), p.62; Edwina Ehrman, *The Wedding Dress: 300 Years of Bridal Fashions* (London 2011), p.179; PAGE 13: "The Bride's Book of Hours," *Vogue* (US), April 1920, pp.63–9; "Beauty for the Bride," *Harper's Bazaar*, May 1952, p.54; "The Bride Never Looked Lovelier . . .," *Vogue* (US), April 1940, p.71; Mary Woodman, *Wedding Etiquette* (London 1966), p.23; PAGE 14: Vera Wang, *On Weddings* (New York 2001), p.236; Madeleine Vionnet, cited in *Fabulous Frocks*, eds. Sarah Gristwood and Jane Eastcoe (London 2008), p.86; Roland Mouret, cited in Amy de la Haye, *A–Z of Style* (London 2011), p.15; PAGE 15: "Discoveries in Chic for the Bride," *Vogue* (US), February 1930, p.94; PAGE 16: *Harper's Bazaar*, March 1958, pp.90–1; "Drawing a Veil Over the Bride," *Vogue* (US), May 1916, pp.43–5; "Discoveries in Chic for the Bride," *Vogue* (US), February 1930, p.94; Ann Lock, *The Complete Guide to Wedding Etiquette* (London

1960), p.102; "Object Matrimony," *Vogue* (US), October 1936, p.89; PAGE 17: Advertisement for Harrods Bridal Boutique in *Brides Magazine*, Summer 1962, p.38; "The Bride's Book of Hours," *Vogue* (US), April 1920, pp.55, 63–9; Marianne Ostier, *Jewels and the Woman: How to Choose and Wear the Correct Jewelry for Every Occasion* (New York 1962), p.132; PAGE 18: G. R. M. Devereaux, *Etiquette for Women* (London 1919), p.94; Anne Edwards and Drusilla Beyfus, *Lady Behave: A Guide to Modern Manners* (London 1956), pp.267–8; "Here Comes the Bride from Paris," *Vogue* (US), May 1916, pp.46–8; "The Bride's Year Book," *Vogue* (US), May 1918, pp.37–44; PAGE 19: Melanie Hicken, "Average wedding bill hits $30,000," money.cnn.com/2014/03/28/pf/average-wedding-cost/, CNN Money, March 28, 2014; Schuyler Velasco, "Wedding cost? Flat. Fewer marry. Wedding boom over?" csmonitor.com/ Business/2012/0604/Wedding-cost-Flat.-Fewer-marry.-Wedding-boom-over, *The Christian Science Monitor*, June 4, 2012

C
See further, Susan Waggoner, *I Do! I Do! From the Veil to the Vows: How Classic Wedding Traditions Came to Be* (New York 2002), pp.94, 106–8; Office for National Statistics, ons.gov.uk/ons/ rel/vsob1/marriages-in-england-and-wales--provisional-/2010/marriages-in-england-and-wales--2010.html (accessed September 14, 2013); PAGE 21: Ann Lock, *The Complete Guide to Wedding Etiquette* (London 1960), p.102; PAGE 22: "Three Toasts to the Bride," *Vogue* (US), April 1941, p.71; "The Wedding Food: Five Menus and a Postscript on Champagne," *Vogue* (US), July 1958, p.95; PAGE 24: "Marry, Marry, Quite Contrary," *Vogue* (US), June 2008, pp.196–8; PAGE 25: Vera Wang, *On Weddings* (New York 2001), p.28; PAGE 26: "Morals for the Married", in Mary Woodman, *Wedding Etiquette* (London 1966), p.7; "The Period Wedding in France," *Vogue* (US), April 1924, p.50

D

PAGE 29: Reem Arca cited from hautecouturista.
blogspot.co.uk (accessed July 26, 2013); PAGE 30:
Marianne Ostier, *Jewels and the Woman: How
to Choose and Wear the Correct Jewelry for Every
Occasion* (New York 1962), p.32; Advertisement
for Elizabeth Arden in *Brides Magazine*, Spring
1962, p.118; Elsa Schiaparelli, cited in *Fabulous
Frocks*, eds. Sarah Gristwood and Jane Eastcoe
(London 2008), p.79; PAGE 31: Vera Wang, *On
Weddings* (New York 2001), p.137; Alexandra
Wentworth, cited in "She's Gotta Have It:
Dressed-down Gown," *Vogue* (US), June 1998,
p.108; "Here Comes the Bride from Paris,"
Vogue (US), May 1916, pp.46–8; "A Guide to
Chic for the Bride," *Vogue* (US), April 1925, p.75;
Justine Picardie, cited in *Fabulous Frocks*, eds.
Sarah Gristwood and Jane Eastcoe (London
2008), p.160; Christian Dior, cited in Amy de
la Haye, *A–Z of Style* (London 2011), p.35; Coco
Chanel, cited in *Fabulous Frocks*, eds. Sarah
Gristwood and Jane Eastcoe (London 2008),
p.175; Norma Shearer, cited in Sinty Stemp,
A–Z of Hollywood Style (London 2012), p.37

E

See further, "The Rules of Engagement," *Vogue*
(US), March 2004, p.378; PAGE 33: Christian
Dior, cited in Amy de la Haye, *The A–Z of Style*
(London 2011), pp.37–8; Diana Vreeland, cited
in Amy de la Haye, *The A–Z of Style* (London
2011), p.38; Yves Saint Laurent, cited in Amy de
la Haye, *The A–Z of Style* (London 2011), p.38;
"Bride of the Year," *Harper's Bazaar*, February
1960, pp.64–5; Genevieve Antoine Dariaux, *A
Guide to Elegance: For Every Woman Who Wants
to Be Well and Properly Dressed on All Occasions*
(London 1964), p.264; Vera Wang, *On Weddings*
(New York 2001), p.25; Franco Moschino, cited
in *Fabulous Frocks*, eds. Sarah Gristwood and
Jane Eastcoe (London 2008), p.103; PAGE 34:
David and Elizabeth Emanuel, *A Dress for

Diana* (London 2006), pp.144, 148, 158; PAGE 35:
"Discoveries in Chic for the Bride," *Vogue* (US),
February 1930, p.95; Marianne Ostier, *Jewels and
the Woman: How to Choose and Wear the Correct
Jewelry for Every Occasion* (New York 1962),
pp.92–4; PAGE 38: "Kiss Me, Kate," *Vogue* (US),
September 2011, pp.676–90, 754–5

F

See further, Susan Waggoner, *I Do! I Do!
From the Veil to the Vows: How Classic Wedding
Traditions Came to Be* (New York 2002), pp.44,
99; PAGE 41: *Harper's Bazaar*, March 1958,
pp.90–1; PAGE 42: "Bride's Lingerie—The Price,
a Pleasant Surprise," *Vogue* (US), April 1952,
pp.144–6; PAGE 43: "Chic for the Bride Who
Marries in Haste," *Vogue* (US), April 1926,
p.96; *Harper's Bazaar*, February 1965, p.53; John
Galliano, cited in *Fabulous Frocks*, eds. Sarah
Gristwood and Jane Eastcoe (London 2008),
p.48; PAGE 45: *Harper's Bazaar*, April 1903, cited
in Cynthia Amnéus, *Wedded Perfection: Two
Centuries of Wedding Gowns* (Cincinnati 2010),
p.291; Suzy Menkes, "Romance in Cascades of
Silk," The *Times*, July 30, 1981, p.2; Vera Wang,
On Weddings (New York 2001), p.138; *Esquire
Fashion Guide for All Occasions*, ed. Frederic
A. Birmingham (New York 1957), p.59; PAGE
46: "The Bride's Year Book," *Vogue* (US), May
1918, pp.37–44; Mrs. Eric Pritchard in *The Cult
of Fashion*, cited in Amy de la Haye, *A–Z of Style*
(London 2011), p.47; Mary Brooks Picken, cited
in Amy de la Haye, *A–Z of Style* (London 2011),
p.47; Valentino, cited in Amy de la Haye, *A–Z
of Style* (London 2011), p.48; "Fashion: Chic for
the Bride Who Marries in Haste," *Vogue* (US),
April 1926, pp.96–7

G

See further, Sheila Rooney, *Century of the
Wedding Dress* (London 1994), pp.4–5, 21; Susan
Waggoner, *I Do! I Do! From the Veil to the Vows:
How Classic Wedding Traditions Came to Be* (New

York 2002), p.98; PAGE 50: Marianne Ostier, *Jewels and the Woman: How to Choose and Wear the Correct Jewelry for Every Occasion* (New York 1962), pp.142–3; PAGE 51: *Esquire Fashion Guide for All Occasions*, ed. Frederic A. Birmingham (New York 1957), p.57; Mary Woodman, *Wedding Etiquette* (London 1966), p.25; PAGES 52 and 53: *Esquire Fashion Guide for All Occasions*, ed. Frederic A. Birmingham (New York 1957), pp.21–2, 57; PAGE 54: Marianne Ostier, *Jewels and the Woman: How to Choose and Wear the Correct Jewelry for Every Occasion* (New York 1962), p.144; "Beauty for the Bride," *Harper's Bazaar*, May 1952, pp.54–9; "The Bride Never Looked Lovelier . . .," *Vogue* (US), April 1940, p.71; *Harper's Bazaar*, February 1960, pp.80–1; PAGE 55: Mary Woodman, *Wedding Etiquette* (London 1966), p.92

H

See further, Susan Waggoner, *I Do! I Do! From the Veil to the Vows: How Classic Wedding Traditions Came to Be* (New York 2002), pp.56, 116–17; Sheila Rooney, *Century of the Wedding Dress* (London 1994), p.37; Charles L. Mo, *To Have and to Hold: 135 Years of Wedding Fashions* (Charlotte, NC 2000), p.45; PAGE 58: "Crowning Glories," *Brides Magazine*, Summer 1962, p.68; "Paris Fashions. Good Taste and Economy. From a Correspondent," The *Times*, March 29, 1920, p.17; Genevieve Antoine Dariaux, *A Guide to Elegance: For Every Woman Who Wants to be Well and Properly Dressed on All Occasions* (London 1964), p.264; "Fashion: Chic for the Bride Who Marries in Haste," *Vogue*, April 1926, pp.96–7; PAGE 59: "Discoveries in Chic for the Bride," *Vogue* (US), February 1930, p.95; PAGE 60: "Paris Fashions. Good Taste and Economy. From a Correspondent," The *Times*, March 29, 1920, p.17; "A Portfolio for the Bride," *Vogue* (US), April 1921, p.39; "Paul Poiret Gowns the April Bride," *Vogue* (US), April 1922, p.58; PAGE

61: *Vogue* 1930 cited in Christina Probert, *Brides in Vogue Since 1910* (London 1984), p.28; PAGE 62: Christina Probert, *Brides in Vogue Since 1910* (London 1984), p.52; *Vogue* 1961 and 1964 cited in Christina Probert, *Brides in Vogue Since 1910* (London 1984), p.62

I

PAGE 65: *Vogue* 1923 cited in Christina Probert, *Brides in Vogue Since 1910* (London 1984), p.16; Vera Wang, *On Weddings* (New York 2001), p.226; PAGE 66: "For the Bride," *Vogue* (US), April 1935, p.85; *Vogue's Book of Etiquette and Good Manners*, 1969, cited in Amy de la Haye, *A–Z of Style* (London 2011), p.62; Mary Woodman, *Wedding Etiquette* (London 1966), p.21

J

PAGE 69: Marianne Ostier, *Jewels and the Woman: How to Choose and Wear the Correct Jewelry for Every Occasion* (New York 1962), pp.92,131; "New Theatre Headdresses," *Vogue* (US), December 1906, p.822

K

See further, Susan Waggoner, *I Do! I Do! From the Veil to the Vows: How Classic Wedding Traditions Came to Be* (New York 2002), p.89

L

PAGE 73: "Discoveries in Chic for the Bride," *Vogue* (US), February 1930, p.95; PAGE 74: Madeleine Ginsburg, *Wedding Dress, 1740–1970* (London 1981), p.12; Edwina Ehrman, *The Wedding Dress: 300 Years of Bridal Fashions* (London 2011), p.27; PAGE 75: "Lingerie for the Bride's Trousseau," *Vogue* (US), April 1919, pp.53, 63; Ann Lock, *The Complete Guide to Wedding Etiquette* (London 1960), p.33; "Lingerie for the Bride's Trousseau," *Vogue* (US), April 1919, pp.53, 63

M

PAGE 78: Advertisement for Lipmans mail-order wedding dresses, *Brides Magazine*, Summer 1962, p.39; "Beauty and the Bride," *Vogue* (US), July 1956, pp.92–3; "Beauty for the Bride," *Harper's Bazaar*, May 1952, pp.54–9; PAGE 79: "The Bride Never Looked Lovelier . . .," *Vogue* (US), April 1940, pp.70–1; "The Parisienne in the Role of Mother of the Bride," *Vogue* (US), April 1921, pp.57–9, 104; PAGE 80: "A Guide to Chic for the Bride," *Vogue* (US), April 1925, p.75; Advertisement for "Bride-Be-Lovely" bridal wear rental service, 66 Cannon Street, Manchester, in *Brides Magazine*, Spring 1962, p.123; PAGE 81: Vera Wang, *On Weddings* (New York 2001), p.249; Marianne Ostier, *Jewels and the Woman: How to Choose and Wear the Correct Jewelry for Every Occasion* (New York 1962), p.132; "Here Comes the Mother of the Bride," *Vogue* (US), August 2001, pp.124–7, 132

N

PAGE 83: "Beauty for the Bride," *Harper's Bazaar*, May 1952, pp.54–9; "The Bride Never Looked Lovelier . . .," *Vogue* (US), April 1940, p.71; Marianne Ostier, *Jewels and the Woman: How to Choose and Wear the Correct Jewelry for Every Occasion* (New York 1962), pp.98–9

O

See further, Mary Woodman, *Wedding Etiquette* (London 1966), p.84; Catherine Woram, *Wedding Dress Style* (London 1993), p.116; PAGE 85: *Youth's Companion*, July 28, 1904, p.357

P

See further, Marianne Ostier, *Jewels and the Woman: How to Choose and Wear the Correct Jewelry for Every Occasion* (New York 1962), p.178; PAGE 87: "Here Comes the Bride from Paris," *Vogue* (US), May 1916, p.46; PAGE 89: "Beauty for the Bride," *Harper's Bazaar*, May

1952, pp.54–9; PAGE 90: "Beauty for the Bride," *Harper's Bazaar*, May 1952, pp.54–9; "The Bride Never Looked Lovelier . . .," *Vogue* (US), April 1940, p.71; PAGE 91: Lady Georgiana Boothby, cited in Christina Probert, *Brides in Vogue Since 1910* (London 1984), p.80; "The Bride Never Looked Lovelier . . .," *Vogue* (US), April 1940, p.71; *Vogue*, 1923, cited in Christina Probert, *Brides in Vogue Since 1910* (London 1984), p.9; Vera Wang, *On Weddings* (New York 2001), p.58

Q

See further, Nigel Arch and Joanna Marschner, *Royal Wedding Dresses from the Royal Ceremonial Dress Collection at Kensington Palace* (London 2003), p.6; Charles L. Mo, *To Have and to Hold: 135 Years of Wedding Fashions* (Charlotte, NC, 2000), p.25; PAGE 93: Marianne Ostier, *Jewels and the Woman: How to Choose and Wear the Correct Jewelry for Every Occasion* (New York 1962), p.131

R

See further, *Brides: Wedding Clothes and Customs 1850–1980* (Liverpool 1980), p.19; Susan Waggoner, *I Do! I Do! From the Veil to the Vows: How Classic Wedding Traditions Came to Be* (New York 2002), pp.21, 24; Catherine Woram, *Wedding Dress Style* (London 1993), pp.52–3; PAGE 95: *Girl's Own Paper* cited in Anthea Jarvis, *Brides: Wedding Clothes and Customs 1850–1980* (Liverpool 1980), pp.9, 20; "Fashion and Beauty: The Bride's Book," *Vogue* (US), May 1951, p.167; *Vogue*, 1950s, cited in Christina Probert, *Brides in Vogue Since 1910* (London 1984), p.52; PAGE 96: "The Bride's Year Book," *Vogue* (US), May 1918, pp.37–44; PAGE 97: Óscar de la Renta, vogue.co.uk/spy/biographies/oscar-de-la-rentabiography (accessed August 7, 2013); PAGE 98: "Discoveries in Chic for the Bride," *Vogue* (US), February 1930, p.95; Marianne Ostier, *Jewels and the Woman: How to Choose and Wear the Correct Jewelry for Every Occasion*

(New York 1962), pp.95, 96; Mary Woodman, *Wedding Etiquette* (London 1966), p.83; PAGE 99: "A Guide to Chic for the Bride," *Vogue* (US), April 1925, p.75; "A Portfolio for the Bride," *Vogue* (US), April 1921, p.38; "Three Toasts to the Bride," *Vogue* (US), April 1941, p.71; Suzy Menkes, "Romance in Cascades of Silk," The *Times*, July 30, 1981, p.2; Edwina Ehrman, *The Wedding Dress: 300 Years of Bridal Fashions* (London 2011), p.10; Vera Wang, *On Weddings* (New York 2001), p.147; PAGE 100: "The Wedding Dress," The *Times*, April 26, 1923, p.vii; PAGE 101: The *Times*, May 7, 1960, cited in Nigel Arch and Joanna Marschner, *Royal Wedding Dresses from the Royal Ceremonial Collection at Kensington Palace* (London 2003), p.29; Julie Burchill, cited in *Fabulous Frocks*, eds. Sarah Gristwood and Jane Eastcoe (London 2008), p.119; Suzy Menkes, "Romance in Cascades of Silk," The *Times*, July 30, 1981, p.2

S

See further, Susan Waggoner, *I Do! I Do! From the Veil to the Vows: How Classic Wedding Traditions Came to Be* (New York 2002), p.30; Catherine Woram, *Wedding Dress Style* (London 1993), pp.42–3; PAGE 103: "Fragrance: The First Fashion a Woman Wears," *Vogue* (US), May 1985, pp.326–33, 363; "Beauty for the Bride," *Harper's Bazaar*, May 1952, pp.54–9; PAGE 104: Vera Wang, *On Weddings* (New York 2001), p.23; "The Bride's Year Book," *Vogue* (US), May 1918, pp.37–44; *Harper's Bazaar*, February 1965, pp.7; PAGE 105: Marlene Dietrich, cited in Sinty Stemp, *A–Z of Hollywood Style* (London 2012), p.100; Ann Lock, *The Complete Guide to Wedding Etiquette* (London 1960), p.39; PAGE 106: "Beauty for the Bride," *Harper's Bazaar*, May 1952, pp.54–9; PAGE 108: Catherine Woram, *Wedding Dress Style* (London 1993), pp.52–3; Madeleine Ginsburg, *Wedding Dress, 1740–1970* (London 1981), *Frocks*, eds. Sarah Gristwood and Jane

Eastcoe (London 2008), p.84; Edith Head, cited in Sinty Stemp, *A–Z of Hollywood Style* (London 2012), p.102; "Paris Fashions. Good Taste and Economy. From a Correspondent," The *Times*, March 29, 1920, p.17; "She's Gotta Have It: Dressed-down Gown," *Vogue* (US), June 1998, p.108; PAGE 109: Vera Wang, *On Weddings* (New York 2001), p.226; PAGE 110: "For the Bride's Day," *Vogue* (US), April 1941, p.65; Vera Wang, *On Weddings* (New York 2001), p.164; Kristie Lau, dailymail.co.uk/femail/article-2160015/Why-bridal-market-flooded-unflattering-strapless-gowns.html, *MailOnline*, June 16, 2012; PAGE 111: Traditional wedding proverbs, cited in Mary Woodman, *Wedding Etiquette* (London 1966), pp.86–9

T

PAGE 113: Vera Wang cited in "Brides Made," *Vogue* (US), December 1990, p.317; *The Etiquette of Marriage* (Halifax 1857), p.22; "Conduct and Carriage or; Rules to Guide a Young Lady on Points of Etiquette and Good Breeding in her Intercourse with the World," *The Ladies' Treasury*, vol. 1 (London 1858), p.239; Vera Wang, *On Weddings* (New York 2001), p.202; PAGE 114: Geoffrey Munn, cited in Amy de la Haye, *A–Z of Style* (London 2011), p.112; PAGE 116: Halston, cited in Amy de la Haye, *A–Z of Style* (London 2011), p.101; PAGE 117: Susan Waggoner, *I Do! I Do! From the Veil to the Vows: How Classic Wedding Traditions Came to Be* (New York 2002), p.28; "The Apparel of the Summer Bride," *Vogue* (US), May 1914, p.27; "Spring Shoe Trousseau for the Bride," *Vogue* (US), April 1940, pp.124–5; "Lingerie for the Bride's Trousseau," *Vogue* (US), April 1919, pp.53, 63; "Fashion: Dressing on a War Income," *Vogue* (US), May 1918, p.59; Ann Lock, *The Complete Guide to Wedding Etiquette* (London 1960), pp.33, 36; "Essays on Etiquette," *Vogue* (US), September 1922, pp.64–5, 104–6

U

PAGE 119: *Esquire Fashion Guide for All Occasions*, ed. Frederic A. Birmingham (New York 1957), p.59

V

See further, Susan Waggoner, *I Do! I Do! From the Veil to the Vows: How Classic Wedding Traditions Came to Be* (New York 2002), pp.53–6; PAGE 121: "Drawing a Veil Over the Bride," *Vogue* (US), May 1916, p.43; *Harper's Bazaar*, February 1965, pp.53–7; Mary Brooks Picken, cited in Amy de la Haye, *A–Z of Style* (London 2011), p.119; "The Bride's Book of Hours," *Vogue* (US), April 1920, p.63; PAGE 123: "The Bride's Year Book," *Vogue* (US), May 1918, pp.37–44; PAGE 124: Vera Wang, *On Weddings* (New York 2001), p.227

W

See further, Sheila Rooney, *Century of the Wedding Dress* (London 1994), p.27; PAGE 130: "A Portfolio for the Bride," *Vogue* (US), April 1921, p.38; Vera Wang, *On Weddings* (New York 2001), p.25; Charles L. Mo, *To Have and to Hold:*

135 Years of Wedding Fashions (Charlotte, NC, 2000), p.13; Madeleine Ginsburg, *Wedding Dress, 1740–1970* (London 1981), p.1; Edwina Ehrman, *The Wedding Dress: 300 Years of Bridal Fashions* (London 2011), p.56; PAGE 131: *Manners and Rules of Good Society, or Solecisms to be Avoided* (London 1902, 26th edition), p.134; "Object Matrimony," *Vogue* (US), October 1936, p.141; "Conduct and Carriage or; Rules to Guide a Young Lady on Points of Etiquette and Good Breeding in her Intercourse with the World," *The Ladies' Treasury*, vol. 1 (London 1858), p.239

X

PAGE 133: "The Nude Bride," *Vogue* (US), January 1998, p.26

Y

PAGE 135: *Vogue* May 1914, cited in Christina Probert, *Brides in Vogue Since 1910* (London 1984), p.8; "Here Comes the Bride from Paris," *Vogue* (US), May 1916, pp.46–8; Marianne Ostier, *Jewels and the Woman: How to Choose and Wear the Correct Jewelry for Every Occasion* (New York 1962), p.133